'Book about' - A fans life with Prince
G Bell

Published 2018 G Bell ong

For my wife, Lorraine and my mother(mam) - the two most important people in my life.

4word	6
Intro	7
Jam 1 – 'Empty Room'	8
Jam 2 - 'Hello'	15
Jam 3 – 'In Love'	18
'The Kid'	18
'Movie Star'	21
Jam 4 – 'Wreka Stow'	23
'Around the World in a Day'	23
'Try my new funk'	27
Jam 5 - 'Days of Wild'	29
'The Morning Papers'	30
'High Fashion'	34
Jam 6 - 'Oh Yeah..'	43
Jam 7 - ' Rock n Roll Love Affair'	54
Jam 8 – 'Collecting Records and Thursdays'	58
Jam 9 - ' One nite alone...Live/Wedding Feast'	77
Jam 10 - 'Goodbye'	127
Outro - 'Welcome to the Dawn'	131
Appendices	137
Sign 'O' the Times - Album playback speech: 01.06.16.	137
Kiss - Prince and the Revolution	140
Live Sets	143

4word

'Makes me wanna cry, thinking about you. 'Beautiful' you said, the way you shook your head'

Much has been written about Prince. Much more will be. Much has been written by Prince. Regrettably, no more will be.

I have written nothing of note, but after months of struggling to come to terms with the death of someone I never met, but can only describe as a man I idolised and adored, and saw as an inspiration and a person I felt love towards, I was compelled to attempt to comprehend why his passing has had such an impact on me, whilst at the same time reflect on the times that Prince Rogers Nelson has been present in my life. How he influenced me and what I can do to fill the void in his absence. Reading fan sites, Prince's death touched many people - his family, his friends, his fellow musicians, and, most notably his legions of fans across the world. Looking through online posts, it did come as some comfort to observe that I was not alone in my grief; and I do class it as grief. Yet this alone could not unravel the deeply profound emotional state I was in for the weeks and months after Prince died, which I kept hidden from most people around me. The purpose of my putting the following thoughts together were multiple - cathartic, nostalgic, but ultimately creative. I wanted, above anything else, to be inspired by Prince and felt compelled to turn my discord into something positive. I had no idea where this would take me, but a sense of achievement and handing something back would, I hoped, be the minimum return. Prince represented a great deal in my life - he came from a different world. A world I could only dream of. But in my dreams, inspired by his words, I would be part of this alternative universe. It's now time to examine our strange relationship.

Intro

'Open your heart, open your mind, a train is leaving all day'

When I first thought of putting my thoughts about Prince together, I was conscious that I didn't want it to be purely about his music and an album by album retrospective. I feel there are better placed journalists and authors who can make a more articulate and comprehensive attempt at this. However, I can't ignore the impact a lot of his songs and albums have had on me; therefore, I would like to share some of these experiences. It's no coincidence that I was at my most impressionable during the mid-eighties, the time Prince was experiencing his most prolific and groundbreaking period. A time known as his 'regal' phase.

Prince released nine albums in the eighties and had countless projects shelved by either himself or his record label. Most notably of these is the 'black' album which was pulled days before its planned release in December 1987 and became one of the most bootlegged albums of all time, until it received an official release in 1994 as part of a contractual obligation when, arguably no one cared. Each Prince album in this period appeared to shift, completely from the previous, almost as if he was casting aside everything he had just learned and wanted to move into a different musical style. He seemed intent on not only out-doing the rest of the pop/rock glitter-arty, but also himself. The ease in which he was able to transcend and recreate became a phenomenon; a feat matched only by the sheer quality of his output. It seemed that barely a year would pass, and a new Prince image and sound were upon us. The leaps he made from 1982's double album '1999' to 1986's 'Parade' would take other artists decades to even come close to. In fact, he made two albums in between, a film, played three tours, not to mention the extra-curricular production, writing, recording, overseeing and participation on albums produced by numerous other artists. He re-defined the term 'prolific' and was often already recording a new album when his current one had just hit the shops. A maestro at work - he could draw from a rich tapestry of influences and yet stamp his own identity on projects. The eighties were his most successful decade, commercially, yes, but there were multi-sellers in the 90's too, where he maintained the same rate of output, and, in fact went on to eclipse his output rate. In the 00's he recognised the potential of the internet, whilst also becoming one of the biggest draws on the 'heritage' circuit, although he was always one step ahead, offering more and pushing boundaries. His final reinvention - being the guitarist in garageband '3rdeyegirl' and simultaneously, taking his vast array of hits on the road via the 'piano and a microphone' world tour, demonstrated that he was hitting yet another creative peak. And yet....

Jam 1 – 'Empty Room'

Thursday April 21st, 2016, 5.58pm. My wife, Lorraine and I have just completed our domestic chore of washing and drying the tea time dishes. We are in the kitchen and begin fooling around with dishcloths in our usual playful, loving way. I am happy. We are happy. I've recently returned to full time work following a lengthy spell of absence recovering from knee surgery, which severely limited my mobility and saw me not leave the house for almost six weeks. The summer is just around the corner. We are looking to plan a holiday and we are having some improvements done to the house. Things seem to be heading in a positive direction.

The house telephone landline is in our front room. It rings. We both, in exaggeration, run into the room. My mobile is situated near the landline and I notice that there are three text messages in a short space of time. They read, 'is it true'? 'What's happened?' And, 'have you heard?' The phone call is from my childhood and close friend Darran who now lives in Edinburgh. Darran and I have been fellow pop music fans (or brothers in pop) since we met in 1983 and experienced many highs and lows together, often linked by a soundtrack. Prince has always been at the pinnacle of our musical admiration. Darran and I are very close, despite the physical distance between our home towns (Darran in Edinburgh, me in Newcastle). We correspond mainly via email and very often the content revolves around our shared Prince experiences, trading off rumours/speculation and our latest finds in music. Often these musical finds, in some way, map back to the world of Prince.

It's unusual for him to phone at this specific time. In fact, it's unusual for him to phone. He sounds upset. Suddenly I'm concerned, and I think about the text messages. He utters in almost a whisper the words I never thought I'd hear, and certainly not at this stage of my life...

"Prince is dead".

I can't understand what I'm hearing and mumble something to him, whilst motioning to Lorraine to change the TV channel. She looks worried for me. I said to Darran I'd speak to him later and I put the phone down. The television news report confirms the sad, sad story and I burst into uncontrollable tears. Facts begin to register - 'died in a lift'...'was found alone'... '911 call from Paisley Park'. The message is clear. PRINCE IS DEAD.

Shock does not come close to describe the feelings and emotions I am rapidly becoming immersed in. Prince had been unwell ten days ago, which forced him to cancel a concert. His private jet had to make an emergency landing somewhere in the US (more on this story would develop over the next few days/months) but there was no indication (or any made public) that anything underlying was present. Prince has always appeared relatively fit for a man of his age and stature. There have been stories about surgery, he walked with a cane. But, again, he was never close to death...Or, was he?

My phone continues buzzing with incoming messages. I don't look at them. I'm too upset. My wife consoles me. I experience a strange sensation that I am a bystander watching my own breakdown. There have been two significant deaths in my life - both family members, both very close. This feels similar...but different. A lot of what happens that night is a bit of a blur. I switch my phone off. I don't want to talk. I just want to cry. I look at various posts on the internet/listen to the radio. I think about music but can't choose to play anything. What on earth could I possibly listen to right now?

Although I opt not to select anything, two songs come into my thoughts, one of which is played at least once on the radio that evening (which I find the only logical medium to have present in the background). The songs are 'Sometimes it snows in April' from the 'Parade' album - the song has always been beautifully sad, but with a hint of a positive slant to it. "All good things they say, never last...and love, isn't love until it's passed". These are the last two lines of the song and, whilst this may be true, it feels extremely poignant tonight given that we are in the month of April.

The other, less obvious song is from Wendy & Lisa's debut (post the 'Revolution' break-up) album and is titled 'Song About'. This song written about the very subject of Prince's extremely successful and well-loved backing band breaking up (it must be said, at Prince's bequest) and begins "Makes me wanna cry, thinking about you".

I cannot think of a better phrase to cover how I am beginning to feel at this moment. Prince, through his music and live performances (and, go on, even his films) brought me and millions more so many thrills, so much joy, so much laughter, so much energy and so much guidance, in one way or another. And now he's not here.

I can do nothing but cry.

Whoopi Goldberg tweets "this is what it sounds like when doves cry". There must be doves crying across the whole world now. I read that various world landmarks are bathed in purple (the colour Prince is most associated with). The television music channels play back-to-back videos, although after a couple of hours it becomes obvious they are all playing the same ten or so clips. The developing story is the lead on most of the news channels. Various people talk about his life, his work and speculate over his death. It all becomes too much. I go to bed at some point, but don't sleep. I think of how it began with Prince, how much he has helped to shape my life and I feel utterly crestfallen that he's dead. I don't give consideration at this moment to his family, his friends or what will happen next.

I feel no better the next day. My wife asks is I should take the day off work, I consider it, but know that I don't have an acceptable, plausible alibi. 'I'm not coming in because Prince died' would not, I think, do me any favours and in a rare moment of rationale I remember that I work in a unit looking to improve outcomes for children with cancer, who may not live to their twenties, let alone the near 58 years of life that Prince experienced.

Switching on my mobile phone and looking at the missed calls/messages I note that via a good friend, the local BBC news team would like to talk to me about Prince. This throws me in a quandary. Is this something I can do? Is it something I should do? In the words of 'International Lover' "Am I qualified?" I'm not a musician, a journalist or a celebrity, but maybe they just want a fans view? I talk it over with my wife and decide that, if practical, I will.

Scanning through the music TV channels, the song 'Purple Rain' is on somewhere. I swiftly flick past it. This song is too emotional to listen to today, even though it is one of Prince's best-known anthems.

On the way into the office, I stop by at the newsagent. All of today's newspapers have Prince on the cover and, very much like the day following David Bowie's death four months earlier, each one has a different image demonstrating the changing faces of Prince through the years. Predictably, the lower end of the tabloid press goes for headlines like 'End of Purple Reign'. Most are respectful, but, again, unsurprisingly I see one tag line that reads something like 'music legend found alone, slumped in lift' and I think "here we go". There has to be an angle for some reporters, doesn't there? I look at all the newspapers and find it heartening that he warrants so much coverage, but I also despair that this only comes about due to his passing. Months later I still have the newspapers, but very few of them have been read.

I don't say a lot to my colleagues at work today, although, to be honest, this is quite normal. I continue to receive text messages, some of which I reply to. My wife is concerned over my state of mind being at work, and moreover, that if I do speak on the radio I will break down.

I manage to get in touch with my friend who works for the local BBC station and we discuss my going on air and conclude that perhaps pre-recording will be a better option to enable anything deemed unsuitable to be edited out prior to broadcast. He also asks me to help him put together a montage of Prince Songs, which I do. However, perhaps 'Sexy MF' would not fit the bill given that this is a mid-morning show...

Surprisingly, I find talking to Anna Foster of BBC Newcastle very easy, and a big relief. I don't think I ramble too much (although once I get started, I feel I perhaps could). The piece is edited and goes to air. I hear it later that night and think it sounds ok, but now I'm thrown - I'm talking about a man I never met, although I spent roughly 20 hours in his 'company'. Yet he inspired me in so many ways. I think back to 1984, where it all began growing up in the West End of Newcastle and how on earth it ever came to this - talking about Prince's death on the BBC.

Initially, as with a lot of high profile deaths, there was a rush to publish/perform tributes to the deceased. Alongside the newspapers which follow the news story, which I buy but don't read in depth, 'special tribute editions' are published of most of the music and style periodicals, which I purchase over the next few months, and also remain, in general, unread - the same going for the US versions my wife brings back from her trip to Las Vegas. They look good, they appear to be very respectful, but they all refer to Prince in the past tense. This is not registering with me. On the radio (April 22nd, 2016), I am referring to Prince in the past tense - me, talking about Prince's life, which is now over. Again, there is the emotion of observing myself doing this - it's not real, is it? Taking a step back, I feel very fortunate that I am asked to do this, but hugely proud. When it comes down to it, I'm only a fan, after all.

At the office on April 22nd, I find that it is not my most productive day at work. During my lunch break I wander aimlessly around the city centre. I don't have my headphones to my MP3 player on. I visit one record shop and they are playing Prince music. I stay and listen to the next track, and the next, thumbing through the Prince CDs - obsessively putting some of them in order of release (I have done this before). Holding the CDs in a record shop, knowing he is dead feels wrong. I don't buy any CDs today.

More coverage continues in the media and it becomes apparent that Prince died alone in a lift in Paisley Park, which was both his home and recording studio - ultimately his playground. This is incredibly upsetting. Death is upsetting, but to learn that a person died with no one nearby - no loved ones, family members or medical professional is unusual, at worst.

That evening I go out for food with my wife and raise my glass to Prince. My wife, as ever, is extremely supportive and understanding of my mood, but at this moment I don't feel sociable.

I am in a confused state of mind - I don't know how to manage this - should I be playing Prince music back to back? Try as I will, I can't begin to choose songs myself - it's just about all I can manage to listen to music that someone else has chosen. Should I be celebrating his life? His impact on mine? None of these seem appropriate, so I mourn the loss. I weep, inconsolably, many times over the weekend, and in the days and weeks to come. There are some sympathetic touches in what I do to help me to absorb some of the coverage. I choose the cover shot from the Guardian Saturday supplement as the image of Prince. I want to remember him by. It's from the mid noughties - he has his eyes closed, and an acceptable amount of make-up applied. He looks stunning, at peace - my perfect vision of how he was at the moment he passed away - the beautiful one. Obviously, this is not how he looked and strikes my wife as quite morbid. Prince had an entrancing stare, which he used to great effect, but his eyes will never be seen again. He will never see again

Over the next few weeks and months I ask myself if it is rational to feel so much sorrow and grief. As I've mentioned, I never met Prince. I've never had a conversation with him. I've never had a pint with him and have certainly never been to his house to watch Dr. Who!

There is a moment in time, in one of my reflective, contemplative moods, when it dawns on me - Prince was in my life for more years than my own father. My dad passed away when I was 27. Prince was very much part of my life from 1984 - 2016 - approaching 32 years. This seems out of sync, but it may help explain why I feel so crushed by Prince's death - perhaps, subconsciously, he became a surrogate father from afar - someone I looked up to for guidance, although where he was when I needed to talk to someone about the amendments to the offside rule in football is a mystery. As are the years of missed pocket money!

I had thought, infrequently (and in the past), that I would make every effort to attend Prince's funeral, should the unthinkable happen. I am now thinking in a thinkable world. It has happened. My wife, in a moment where I am at one of my low points says she would understand if I wanted to go. As much as I would want to be there, I don't think that I could hold myself together. I have attended the funerals of both my father and my grandmother - both people were extremely close to me and their deaths were a huge shock - I think of them both every day and long for their return. At each service, I feel I kept my emotions under wraps, out of respect, out of duty. With Prince I feel it would be different. Truthfully, I suspect that there will be no public service, and this is indeed confirmed. His remains are cremated in a private service just days after his death, in keeping with his religious beliefs. This is very appropriate. Prince filled many roles to many people and he had a close group of friends, along with family. They should be allowed to respectfully mourn as much as possible away from the glare of the media and fans - including me. Following the service, a fragile looking Sheila E speaks to several fans. This means a lot to me, from afar. Later Sheila would write a song about her feelings and experience of knowing Prince. I admire her even more for doing this and for presenting it to the public, when she should still have been suffering enormous grief over the loss of a very close friend.

It is almost two weeks into a world without Prince. The tributes, in the main, have stopped. There is no official confirmation of the cause of death, although there are reports of an addiction to prescription pain killers, brought on by the athletic stage performances in the 80's, all carried out while wearing high heeled shoes. I am listening to some music - not yet Prince's. I listen to two albums only and pretty much nothing else - it is almost akin to a 'safe zone' knowing that I won't react to any of the tracks I listen to. This is a start and is a step forward from wearing my MP3 headphones without the player being turned on, as was the case for almost 2 weeks. The next step is to listen to Prince's music. I plan this and conclude that a staged approach is best. Instrumentals first - 'Alexa de Paris' - the B-side to 'Mountains' and featured in the film 'Under the Cherry Moon'. The track is a mesmerising guitar driven tune, lifted to a crescendo by a heavy drum solo. I have this track as part of my wedding intro music - the music that is being played as guests turn up and I try to remain calm, waiting for my soon to be wife to arrive. Amongst this 'wedding intro' compilation, which I put together myself (or playlist as I believe it is termed in the modern vernacular) Prince or Prince related instrumentals feature heavily - tracks from the 'C-Note' album, some of the Madhouse work, Venus de Milo, and the 'love theme' from Purple Rain, 'God'. Thankfully while listening to this music, for the first time since Prince's death, I can still recount an extremely happy wedding day, although there is more than a hint of me returning to Prince and his passing, and perhaps what may have been played at his funeral.

Having overcome the first stage or reentry into Prince's musical world, I consider how I will begin to listen to his vocal tracks. This has to be pure and it has to be something I do alone. In the main, this is how I have listened to Prince's albums - with no-one else present. There have been occasions, sure, when communally I have enjoyed the listening experience of a Prince album - generally with close friends, and one occasion as part of a record listening collective. Perhaps this is one reason why losing Prince feels so personal. Like I knew him. Like each album was his personal message to me. There have been times, I have to admit whereby some form of ESP, I have felt that Prince communicated with me. I am very aware of how absurd that reads, and I am sure everyone who was or is fanatical about a pop star/movie star/politician/sports hero has had 'moments' like this, but whether it be through his songs, or the perceived way he has glanced my way at a concert, Prince has had that effect on me.

There is a very significant scene in Under the Cherry Moon, and (spoiler alert), it did turn out to be prophetic. The character that Prince plays is shot dead towards the end of the film. His final words to his romantic link before dying are 'we had fun, didn't we?' No truer a set of words could he leave us with - Prince provided me (and countless others) with hours of fun, amongst many other emotions, and, if in some bizarre way those were his last words before his death (not that I would particularly like to know), he spoke from the heart.

As a footnote to this chapter, one absolute mind crusher is the short film 'Hometown Hero' - this is sent to me by Darran and is a beautiful tribute from the people of Minneapolis to one of their own. Here, I get a sense of what Prince meant to the community of Minneapolis, and how proud he made that community feel - more so that he never moved away, even dismissing the cold weather as a positive in that 'it keeps the bad people out'. I learn a lot about Prince that I didn't already know from this short clip and it is quite heartwarming to feel the love. It is also incredibly upsetting (again) that we are referring to Prince in the past tense. However, the sucker punch is finding out, right at the end of the film that 'Sometimes it snows in April' was recorded in 1985...on April the 21st, exactly 31 years to the day of his death ('Life could be so nice was also recorded on this day). I'm not a great believer in conspiracy theories, and I can't feel that Prince planned to record a song he had written about the pain of loss on the day we would lose him, but it does fit with my romantic ideals of the man. All good things they say, never last.

Looking back, I begin to think about how I became this involved in his Paisley world, to the extent that I mourn his loss on a level that I have only done for close family. I have to go back to my childhood - something I do on a regular basis - to remember when Prince wasn't in my life, and the impact he had on my youthful years, which, ultimately have helped shape me - good or bad - into the person I am now.

Jam 2 - 'Hello'

My fledgling obsession with pop music began, dependent on the yearly album I would be given by my parents/grandparents at Christmas, or singles on 'special occasions', which I don't recall really having much of a choice over. In my early years, these were nursery rhyme records and bizarrely, 'I'm the leader of the gang' by Gary Glitter (no more to be said about this, other than 'who knew??). My obsession with all things 'Star Wars' and sci-fi as a 5-year-old led to the soundtracks of the films finding their way into my budding vinyl collection. However, the first pop star I became obsessed with, and was afforded the luxury of having his album bought for me was Adam Ant - then front man of the chart topping 'Adam and the Ants.'

Adam was a true pop star, although it wasn't an overnight success. He worked his way through pub rock and then punk rock, issued an awkward, but utterly absorbing debut album with the Antz (note spelling) 'Dirk Wears White Sox'. This is an album I would come to later, but remains a firm favourite due to its raw, angular aggression and broody darkness. It's definitely not pop - or not as we know (or knew) it, and certainly didn't trouble the mainstream charts, which, ultimately meant I had no knowledge of Adam or his Ants (note spelling) until the next album, released with a different lineup and a much more radio friendly sound. 'Dog Eat Dog', 'Kings of the Wild Frontier' and 'Ant Music' all hit the Top 40 in 1980 and saw me, at the dizzy heights of eight, fall for this swashbuckling twin drummer beat, just as I was meant to. Adam had a very clever, calculated plan and wanted to achieve mass appeal from 8 to 80. He might have been slightly off putting with his Red Indian (Native American) war paint, but this was quite conservative around the era of men wearing full makeup, just as Bowie and Bolan had ten years earlier.

Dressing up was very much back in vogue and this mirrored a lot of Adam's songs, which, themselves painted vivid pictures, pictures that let dreamers (like me) dream. Adam came as a perfect pop package - stylish, provocative, intelligent, adventurous, witty and able to project ideas to the masses. He was also good looking and extremely hard working. It seemed that you couldn't turn on the television/radio or pick up a newspaper/magazine without seeing him. He was marketed very well, feeling equally comfortable in the pages of 'Record Mirror' and 'Smash Hits'. He used the new music video medium to the max, where the visions in his (and the listener's) head were given the opportunity to come to life; not least in the two number one singles from the 'Prince Charming' album, 'Stand and deliver' and 'Prince Charming' itself.

The Prince Charming single was particularly notable as my dad bought it for me. Records were not easy to come by for my sister and me, at least not ones we wanted (subconsciously or not). Part of that was financial - we didn't get enough pocket money to buy a single, let alone an album. I don't actually recall asking for any records to be honest, but on occasions such as birthdays and Christmas we would be afforded something like

'The Wombles' or 'The Smurfs' or a soundtrack such as Star Wars and Grease in successive years! This would occasionally include pop 'hits' like a couple of David Essex singles, which I liked, for amongst other reasons because they were on the same record label as the Wombles. 'Window', the B-side to 'Gonna Make You a Star' still provokes a level of unnerving fear and terror in me to this day with its 'Mommy, I'm scared' outro.

Another reason that record purchases were at the bequest of my parents and grandparents at that time was availability. Records were sold in record shops or record departments and pretty much nowhere else. Supermarkets sold food, petrol stations sold petrol (and Smurfs), and there was no sign of the internet to download. So, record shops it was, although they were clearly not deemed the sort of place that a pre-10-year-old and his younger sister were to frequent. Therefore, one day in 1981 on his return from work, my dad presented me with the 7-inch Adam and the Ants single 'Prince Charming' (ironically, very fitting given the subject that I am writing about). My sister Margaret, got 'Green Door' by Shakin' Stevens, though I'm not sure whether she liked it. This was a revolution - 45 revolutions to be exact. Amongst other things, it showed that my parents were noticing my interest in pop. It also showed there had to be parity. My sister had to have something when I did. It also demonstrated clearly that my dad had a bit too much spare time during his working day.

Over the years, the song 'Prince Charming' has come in for some undue criticism. It was very different to all of Adam's previous hits, as it was more 'mid-tempo'. It began with a shriek, and whilst it's layers built, the theatrics developed and the refrain 'ridicule is nothing to be scared of' became a mantra. Arguably, this was part of Adam's plan. Here was a man not scared to dress up, wear makeup, have his image on a line of products (I loved the Adam stationary) or have a 'custard pie' in his face on popular anarchic Saturday morning television show 'Tiswas'. Also, the imagery was again, very strong. The 'Prince Charming' character was a mash up of satin, fancy frills and feminine grace. The polar opposite to the dandy highwayman of Stand and Deliver'.

Top of The Pops showed the video for the song following its debut at Number 2. What a video! With its pantomime theme, contemporary choreography, Diana Dors as the fairy godmother and Adam playing his heroes towards the end. I loved it all, and the fact that this was recognised by the gift of an actual copy of the single was observant. Ok, so it wasn't in a picture sleeve, but it was thrilling nonetheless. Later that year, for Christmas, my sister was given the current Shakin Stevens album and I got the 'Prince Charming' album in its full colour, gatefold sleeve glory! Admittedly, this album has worn less well than 'Kings' or 'Dirk', in fact, it wasn't even that good at the time, and the subsequent reviews I have read are not too complimentary. But it did have 'Stand and Deliver' on and 'Prince Charming', so it wasn't all bad.

Eventually Adam would disappear from the charts in the mid-nineties having only made fleeting appearances in that decade and had dropped off the social circuit completely by the early noughties, only to re-emerge in a particularly upsetting incident which unveiled his diagnosis of bipolar disorder. It was with huge pride that I finally got to see Adam perform a concert in full in 2011 (I had met him at an in-store signing in 1995 where he performed three acoustic numbers). I have seen Adam a number of times in concert and always feel thrilled to see him. He is still clearly battling his demons, which is quite apparent at times. However, the voice is still there as well as that sprinkling of stardust that first attracted me as an 'Ant fan'.

Whilst I was still a couple of years away from the start of my 'pop consumerism', Adam was the one who started it all off, and as I would learn, in the world of pop and pop fanism, and as a Prince fan, ridicule is truly nothing to be scared of!

***

As grateful as I was to the gifting of records, I decided by 1983 that it was time that I made my own way in the world of purchasing vinyl. My early self-purchases were all singles. Seven-inch singles to be precise. The first two were both bought on the same day; 'Breakaway' by Tracey Ullman (a Number 2 hit) and 'Is there something I should know?' By Duran Duran (their first Number 1). Both were on their way down the charts, both came in picture sleeves, and both were bought from the conservative retail point of WH Smiths in the centre of Newcastle. I went to the shop on my own, after school (quite daring for an 11-year-old, but with parental consent) and paid for them with my own money - well the money my parents had donated to me as 'pocket money'. I loved having 'my own' records; looking over the covers for information, reading the credits on the label and playing both the 'A' and 'B' sides in my bedroom on the record player my parents had bought for me. They probably never thought where this seemingly routine purchase would lead me. Yes, I had a bike, yes, I had a snooker table, a dartboard, numerous Star Wars toys and comics, but my record player was my true love.

Jam 3 – 'In Love'

It was 1983 and I was 11 years old when I first heard of Prince. He had been a recording artist for 5 years at that point. Nevertheless, an 8-year-old wouldn't (and shouldn't) be exposed to the topics Prince sung about in some of his early songs. Just about everything on the 1980 album 'Dirty Mind' for example. The first I ever heard of his music was actually an instrumental version of the then (very) minor hit '1999'. This was used by Radio 1 DJ Gary Davies as background music during the weekly top 40 singles chart run down, although I didn't really know it. I seem to recall the lyrics for the song were also printed in 'Number 1' magazine, with a picture of him in full in Purple trench coat mode. Again, this didn't particularly register.

1984 was the year that catapulted Prince to mega stardom with huge hit singles from the multi-million selling album 'Purple Rain' which sound tracked the smash hit film of the same name. The lead single from the album, and actually the last song written for the project was 'When Doves Cry'. This was the song that got me interested in Prince; his sound, his image, his style, his imagination, his depth, his sensitivity, his genius. Pretty deep thinking for a 12-year-old! The song was one of many that filled the airwaves during the glorious summer of pop in 1984. This was the summer where Wham! Duran Duran and, most notably, Frankie Goes to Hollywood dominated the charts. I loved it all, but from nowhere came 'When Doves Cry'. I was instantly intrigued by the originality and mystery, the complex simplicity. I was hooked. It demonstrated depth yet sounded sparse with the Linn drum (Prince's signature effect from the period) being the prominent instrument. The track drew me in and made me ask the question, "What sounds it like when doves cry? That beautiful analogy that takes you to the very limit of heartbreak; the line used by Whoopi Goldberg to describe how she felt upon hearing of Prince's death.

'The Kid'

My parents owned houses and flats (upstairs/downstairs) where we first lived, which when sold in 1983, permitted us to move to a bigger house (a semi-detached) in a slightly better area in the West End of Newcastle. A few years prior to this, when it came to the age where my sister and I could no longer realistically share a bedroom, they also were able to spend money on converting our loft into two separate bedrooms. This made us feel special. Our own bedrooms, above the entire street. An orbit of discovery and, for me, safety with my records. As a family, we always had at least one week in the summer when we 'went on holiday', which, back then meant a week in Scarborough or the Lake District. Simple British holidays. This may have lacked the climatic heat of the more glamorous continental locations that are visited as the norm for summer holidays today, but these were, by and large, not within reach of the average working-class family in 1970's England.

It was during one of these trips that I experienced my 'first summer of pop' when my dad rented a car to use for two weeks in the summer. This was quite normal practice and something we looked forward to every year. This particular year (1984) for the first time the car came with a radio! Maybe the previous year's cars did have a radio, maybe it just wasn't used. Maybe I just wasn't paying attention. Maybe my dad chose not to have Radio 1 on. But all of that changed this year. For me, 1984 was the dawn of listening to pop music. It seemed there was no end to the hits in the top 40 which had appeal to me. It's hard to say if my parents were aware of how much I was absorbing from the radio on our long trips in the car that summer (I particularly recall a day trip to Liverpool to visit the national garden festival that year), but absorb I did, particularly as it wouldn't be uncommon to hear the same song two or three times in a round trip. I have an awful lot to thank my parents for, in the way they helped to shape my life and influence the person I have become. But I suspect they are (or were) completely unaware of the impact Prince would have on my life, and certainly would be oblivious to the fact that the songs on the radio that summer of 1984 would influence me and change my musical tastes forever, even in the way I thought from hereon in. But this is indeed where Prince first came along with 'When Doves Cry'. This was also a time when the music video was in relative early and experimental stages, yet the clip used to promote 'When Doves Cry' again seemed like it came from a different world. It appeared full of mystery and it didn't quite resonate initially with me that it was actually from a film.

Best heard in its full-length version (coming in at 5 minutes 52 seconds) and even better viewed in long format video, this song would begin my fascination with Prince. He looked out of line with the other pop stars of the time; exotic, enigmatic and brooding. Operating in his own world, which there were glimpses of, intercut with snatches of the Purple Rain film throughout the video, as well as a performance shot in a completely white room featuring all of the Revolution. To me, this didn't represent Prince and his band in a studio making a promo video, it was an insight into how he lived his life. He didn't do 'off stage/on stage' - this was it 24-7. His house, in my mind, would have a room with no furniture, just a spiral staircase, where the Revolution were always present, waiting for his next inspired move. Some years later I would view out-take stills from a photo shoot of that era, which were fascinating, but also kind of broke my vision that Prince and the band were just standing in that room, hanging out, writing songs, thinking, musing, creating, when a photographer just happened to pop by and capture a candid moment - as unrealistic as that vision was!

I bought the When Doves Cry single in the summer of 1984 as it rose up the pop charts to peak at Number 4 in the UK, representing Prince's first Top 10 hit in this country. It was a slow burner and climbed the top 40 steadily, as the song gained momentum with more and more airplay. Paying the sum of £1.99 for the 12-inch version, I was captivated by the mystique of the cover. No words were present on the front, just a grainy still of Prince's face. He appeared to be wearing a white shirt, perhaps a coat, or was it a cape? Large sunglasses covered his eyes. Not a lot was given away via the front of the cover, but a lot of intrigue ensued. The reverse was a little more unveiling in that the titles of the two songs on the release and the artist band name were displayed against a backdrop of colourful flowers. The text was set out in a very artistic font, coloured purple. The B-side of the song was noted as '17 Days' with the incredible and extremely long subtitle (The rain will come down, then U will have 2 choose. If U believe, look 2 the dawn and U shall never lose). The centre of the record itself echoed these graphics. It was notable that the release was credited to 'Prince and the Revolution' although the song 'When Doves Cry' has writing credits only associated with Prince.

Listening to the full-length version of 'When Doves Cry' in my bedroom in 1984, I was taken aback with how much more there was to the song that I hadn't already heard. I was, at this stage of my music buying life, coming to terms with the depth afforded to the 12-inch single. The chance to expand/extend/transform, or, on some occasions, ruin a song with extra verses/instrumentation/production. Thankfully When Doves Cry was far from ruined. The whole track made so much more sense in its longer format; more emotion, more intensity and a full guitar solo. The song also ended perfectly with a keyboard run, instead of the 7-inch fade out. Years later, I would discover that a full version video existed, which was mind blowing, if for nothing more than begging the question 'why hasn't this been shown before'?

There was much more to Prince the performer, the artistic visionary, the star, than just occasional pop hits. Lyrically, this song was very much bathed in sadness, as is Prince at the beginning of the video. It sees Prince reminiscing over a love that is in turmoil, but his use of language to describe a fairly mundane scenario is quite vivid and romantic, yet slightly distressing;

> 'Animals strike curious poses, they feel the heat, the heat between me and you...How could you just leave me standing alone in a world so cold? Why do we scream at each other? This is what it sounds like When Doves Cry'.

The likening of Prince's pain to an assumed sound of doves crying is mysterious yet beautiful. Dark and light at the same time. The track is very much a hurting and haunting tale backed by the sparse rhythm of the Linn drum, whilst the much-mentioned lack of a bass line renders it a true original. I had heard nothing like it before, and I was pretty sure no one else had. As I would later discover, it did build on the 'Prince sound', but even within that soon to be labelled genre; When Doves Cry is a stand out.

If anything, the B-side is arguably better. Another bittersweet, Linn drum driven track. '17 days' maybe doesn't have the mystique of 'When Doves Cry' but it certainly has the hooks, the rhythm, the melody, the breakdown and that trademark Prince sound. Beautifully backed (and credited) by the Revolution. It has to be said this track is almost wasted as a B-side. I would later discover, this was not unusual for Prince in the era where singles had two sides to fill. Both songs have really strong memories and paint very vivid pictures of Prince in a supremely creative mode, pushing the boundaries of popular music, both using, and, at the same time creating new styles by mixing up rock and pop with funk and soul. Indeed, I think it's fair to say that' When Doves Cry' could easily have been a ballad, and on occasions, it has been performed in such a way, although not to my knowledge by Prince. 'When Doves Cry' pushed the door open for me to Prince's world. It was a world that certainly wasn't cold, but it was a world that would eventually leave me feeling alone.

'Movie Star'

The remainder of 1984 became Prince's year, more so in his native America, but there was still plenty of 'purpleness' offered to the UK and I took it all! 'Purple Rain' was released as a single and hit Number 8 in the British charts. The UK 7-inch edit did not do the song justice at all, and therefore, I didn't fall in love with it at first listen. It wasn't until I received a copy of the 12-inch 'long version' on tape (from Darran), that I began to appreciate the anthem it was. I have tried to quantify the enormity of this epic track, looking to what fundamentally this song does and why, still now, it reduces me to tears. I think Prince simply nailed it. Whether he was writing the song with the film in mind, or, writing it for another artist, it does feel like he poured so much of his heart and soul into the track. It's often forgotten that the song actually doesn't close the movie - most likely as there is too much sorrow and anguish contained therein to end the film on a downer. The song begins simply and recognisable enough, and introduces Prince's apologetic vocal, softly, almost as if he is in an empty room, or metaphorically an empty soul. His skill in building the song to its crescendo is phenomenal - the song draws you in, to the point where there just has to be an outpouring. The fact that Prince explained the lyric as pertaining to being with the one you love at the end of the world gives the song added depth.

Many people choose to perform 'Purple Rain' in tribute to Prince following his death, but no one comes close to capturing the emotion he displayed every time I saw him perform the song. It is the track that arguably defines Prince on a mass scale and the track I struggle with listening to most of all in the aftermath of his passing. It is a song laced with emotion at the best of times, particularly when viewed in the context of the accompanying film, and every time I hear or see it in the immediate days after 'April 21st', I breakdown. The tidal wave of heartache combined with triumph that hits you when Prince adlibs following the guitar solo, breaks my heart, almost literally. It may be a song that he, at times, tired of playing, but to know he will never perform it again, chokes me up.

I don't hear the Purple Rain album until around Christmas 84 via a copied version on tape (again, from Darran). The single 'I would Die 4U' was released but didn't hit the UK top 40. I acquire the 12-inch of the single in a bargain bin from Woolworths and become fascinated with the two tracks on the B-side - 'Another Lonely Christmas' and 'Free'. Both ballads, but very different to each other. I notice that the text next to 'Free' informs me that the song is from the 1999 album, and I now begin to understand and have an appreciation of Prince's vast back catalogue.

I won't own the Purple Rain album for a good few months yet, but on hearing my copied version, I see that there are many strings to Prince's bow. Every track has a killer and very personal opening line from 'Dearly beloved, we are gathered here today', through to 'Where is my love life', and finally, to 'I never meant to cause you any sorrow'. Prince is being very open and candid with his feelings and emotions but given that the album also represents part of the soundtrack to the film. It is extremely plausible that Prince is writing in character. As an album, 'Purple Rain' is packaged and sequenced perfectly for pop consumption and aimed at world domination. The sound is radio friendly, yet at the same time quite challenging. It has elements of funk and soul, but new layers in the shape of the keyboard and Linn drum added in and mixed with quite heavy guitar. It is often argued that Prince went for a hugely commercial sound to captivate a 'whiter' audience. Whatever the rights and wrongs of this were, it certainly worked. Purple Rain the song, the album, the film and the subsequent US tour made Prince into a household name and catapulted him from cult artist to mega stardom on the level of Michael Jackson.

As much as Prince was the star in Purple Rain, Morris Day and The Time did a very good attempt to steal his thunder. An over the top exaggeration of his persona, perhaps, but The Time were funky as hell and showed a white working class 12-year-old male like me, what soul/funk meant. I had never seen a man of colour holding court so masterfully as Morris Day. Yes, there was Eddie Murphy at that time, but he was a comedian. His was an act. This seemed to be Morris being Morris. The moves he showed on the stage were not far from The Time's live act, as I would discover in later years, and he had some killer lines. Admittedly, there was some quite derogatory comments/acts towards women, which should not be overlooked, but Prince would later defend the script - although not the acting! The Purple Rain film is one I adore to this day and rank it amongst my favourites. It is certainly not the best film ever made but is one of the better music films. This is largely to do with the tightly shot concert footage inserted throughout and the strong, camp streetwiseness of Morris. Oh, and Prince is in it!

Jam 4 – 'Wreka Stow'

'Around the World in a Day'

The very first Prince album I bought with my own money was 'Around the World in a Day'. The lead up to its release in April 1985 was pretty subdued, but it landed in the middle of a hive of activity (not for the first time) in Prince's career. Since the release of 'When Doves Cry' in the summer of 1984, there were three further singles from the 'Purple Rain' album (each with a non-album B-Side). There was the album itself, a re-released double A-side featuring '1999' and 'Little Red Corvette' in January 85, Prince's contribution to the USA for Africa project ('4 the tears in your eyes'), as well as the associated artists albums, which were to varying degrees, essentially Prince projects fronted by a variety of Minneapolis funksters completing a lot of Princely goodness to digest. Some of these extra-curricular albums I wouldn't fully appreciate until a little further down the line (funds to buy all of this product were, more often than not, the limiting factor), but as The Time and Apollonia 6 both featured in the 'Purple Rain' film (although not the released soundtrack) it was quite easy to appreciate that there was more than the 'Prince and the Revolution' albums' coming out of Minneapolis.

During this period, a large part of the world became seduced by Prince, but that wasn't difficult. He was featured in a variety of magazines from the heavy metal 'Kerrang' to the serious music papers, such as US 'heavy' 'Rolling Stone' and the UK pop market in the form of 'Smash hits' and 'Number 1'. He got his own 'Spitting Image' puppet, was sent up by Lenny Henry and mocked by the British tabloid press following his appearance at the British Phonographic Industry awards (forerunner to the Brits) in February 1985 where he accepted two awards accompanied by his minder 'Big Chick' and muttered in a softly spoken voice 'All thanks to God'. This appearance alone showed a much softer side to Prince; a vulnerability, yet also a confidence to bring his world into the mainstream.

This confidence was very clear with the release in April 1985 of 'Around the world in a Day'. So confident was Prince in the belief of his new album off the back of Purple Rain, it was released without any forerunning single or video, or indeed any promotion. There was an advert in the UK music press, but again, this gave little away. There is an urban legend (one of many) that surrounds Prince's presentation of the album to his record label (Warner's) that describes how Prince, surrounded by his entourage and carrying flowers, which were liberally dispersed out into the room, said nothing before, during or after the playback. The record label corporate suits that were present, were all gearing up for 'Purple Rain II' and were somewhat gob smacked that this was so far from it. This was Prince doing what Prince does (or did) best - the unexpected. He had delivered (very much ahead of schedule) an album that took a new direction with few tracks screaming 'hit single'. Not exactly music to the label's ears, so to speak.

At the end of the recently completed 'Purple Rain' tour, Prince had also announced his 'retirement' from live shows as he was going to look for the 'ladder' (a tie in with the penultimate track on the ATWIAD album). Remember, it wasn't even a year since the 'Purple Rain' album had been released, but Prince was clearly not intending to live on his past success despite the record company presumably preferring more live shows and a couple more singles from the current album to push sales further. This was not for Prince. ATWIAD was actually being recorded during 'days off' on the Purple Rain tour. He clearly worked fast, and didn't stand still, physically or metaphorically. The album sold well, but it was no 'Purple Rain'. For me, this was my first taste of Prince the auteur - the creative workaholic, the magician who had a thousand tricks up his sleeve.

I got wind of the album release and convinced myself I needed to hear it as soon as possible. This would mean saving (or getting an advance) of two weeks pocket money. The album was priced around £3.99/£4.49 and I got £2.50 a week which meant I would need to borrow the money. Thankfully my parents understood, as they would numerous times over the years. Indeed, I can recall my mother quite clearly remarking while I was watching the 1999 video on Top of the Pops in early 1985 that I 'liked him'. Clearly my fascination with Prince was evident to my family early on, although perhaps the depth of this wasn't something they were prepared for!

So, the album purchase 'loan' was secured and I had planned when I would make the journey to Newcastle town centre to buy the record. It had to be a Saturday as that was generally when I got my pocket money. I wasn't quite tuned in to the fact that records were released and available on a Monday as yet. So, on Saturday morning I got the number 12 bus into town and hastily walked to the HMV branch in Northumberland Street. And, there I saw it. The album sleeve stuck out a mile as it was so colourful. The artwork was a kaleidoscope of characters, some of which I would learn upon listening bore direct reference to the songs. It was very noticeable that the title of the album was printed onto a sticker which was pressed over the album cover, almost as if it was an afterthought. This technique was something I would see used on many of Prince's albums to come. It was almost as if someone had told Prince that you need the title somewhere on the front cover. He had refused, so the sticker became a compromise. When opened out, the album sleeve of ATWIAD represents a great piece of art and I can see why Prince and the sleeve designer would not want to tarnish this with potentially distracting text.

I looked at the song titles in eagerness and anticipated what they may sound like. Would they be like 'Purple Rain' which, at this point was still the only Prince album I had heard? There wasn't really a lot given away. Perhaps 'Condition of the Heart' was a ballad? Or maybe it was a rap about someone suffering from angina? I devoured the sleeve, looking for clues, trying to spot Prince and the band amongst those depicted. Maybe he was there. Maybe Wendy and Lisa were. Maybe not. The colours of the sleeve were incredibly striking, and it did make the album jump up and scream amongst its contemporary releases on the racks in HMV. I paid the money and hastily made my way back to the bus stop to start my journey home, clutching my newly purchased album. Less than a fiver may not seem a lot, but this was quite a moment in my life. It was the first time I had gone to buy an album on my own and with my own money (sort of). Albums were not the norm for teenagers to buy, they were too expensive and, more often than not, also a bit of an effort to listen to. My only previous experiences of buying albums from record shops were when I had been given a record token and my mother agreed to take me to buy a Duran Duran album. These occasions had to be supervised due to potential complications. Other big hitting albums of the time, had, in the main been bought for me or via the aforementioned tokens. They included Welcome to the Pleasure Dome, Arena, Make it Big, and the Adam and the Ants albums, but going to buy Around the World in a Day was the first time I had bought a brand new release without hearing a note of it. This filled me with nervous excitement and anticipation; however, there was also a sense of doubt. What if it's rubbish? I've spent two weeks of pocket money - No sweets or comics for two weeks. Oh dear!

This fact wasn't lost on a friend I encountered on the bus journey back home, who, when learning that I had bought the album, questioned if I had heard any of the songs. When I replied 'no', he gave me a disgruntled look and asked, 'so what did you do that for', or words to that effect. At this point I actually thought, isn't that the point? Even if it is nine tracks of dirge, it's new. I've never heard it before - it's a voyage of discovery. To this day I am still very proud of myself for taking this calculated gamble. It paved the way for me and I often think back in a 'what if' sort of reflection. I also think that in 1985 it was a relatively bold move for a 13-year-old to make. But Prince had chosen me. This is the way I have looked at my fascination and connection with him and his music. I didn't choose to follow him, he selected me as a follower and 'Around the world in a Day' was just the beginning.

'Open your heart, open your mind' is the opening line to the title track of the album and it could not have been more perfect, for Prince and for me. It did exactly that. Building on the framework of Purple Rain, ATWIAD added futuristic retro Minneapolis psychedelia in the title track. The second was the lead UK single 'Paisley Park'. This is a place, which Prince told me, in my heart. Even now, I can be taken away to another world by the opening two tracks. Prince had created a parallel universe by the medium of sound where dreams were played out to a funk soundtrack with liberal sprinklings of heavy guitar awash with Paisley psychedelia. Certain critics and record execs didn't care for the vast departure from 'Purple Rain', but structurally the albums are tremendously similar Both have nine tracks, both have a killer heartbreak song at track three and both have an eight minute plus epic. 'The Ladder' is extremely similar in rhythm to 'Purple Rain' – Or, is it just me??

The content of the songs, however, is very different; less personal, more recitals and more imaginative, but brought round to an exceptional summary of a way of thinking - 'life it ain't too funky, unless it's got that pop'. I took it that Prince was not referencing cream soda here! The sonic soundscapes and layered textures made his album a voyage of discovery. Each track unlocking unique abstract rhythmic 'funktional' shapes.

As with most Prince Albums, it is difficult to pick out a favourite track. This becomes very changeable and can fluctuate with my mood, settings, etc. I wouldn't particularly want to recite every lyric from every song, but at the time of writing, two tracks do stand out. 'Condition of the Heart' is a piece of absolute beauty. Prince's vocal range sweeps and soars, conveying genuine heartbreak in only the way he can, although there is the sense that this is perhaps not his own. He is telling the story of two people who have inhabited the world that the album references. It is part of a journey we are on with Captain Prince at the helm. 'Condition of the Heart' also introduced the name 'Clara Bow' to me. This was something Prince would do liberally throughout his career, referring to cultural and contemporary figures; literally or by wearing influences on his sleeve. It was as if he was, amongst many other roles, acting as teacher. Unlike the tutors at school, I wanted to listen - I wanted to learn, and was eager to do so. There's a very unconventional opening to the track, almost as if there is a suffix to it. The opening piano section plays like a mini concerto, and displays Prince's clear talent with the instrument, being amongst the first of many he mastered.

The other track to mention, is 'Tambourine' because of its lack of convention. There are screams and shouts in the vocals, a frenzied bassline and almost improvised drums. But it works. Again, it sounds like nothing before and since and could easily have been a B-side. (The B-sides to the singles from this era were at times, sublime – think about 'She's Always in my Hair' and 'Hello') - yet it fits perfectly into the wider picture of the album, readying us for the rock/pop opener of side 2's 'America'. 'Tambourine' is quite a challenge to listen to and it does have an element of being a 'sketch' of a song, but maybe that's what I like about it. I don't think I would want to hear a later version if one actually exists. I liked the way my ears were being re-educated by Mr. Nelson and this feeling would very much continue!

I liked the gathering of momentum I had experienced when thinking about buying the album and subsequently the thrill of getting it home and hearing a whole new set of songs from Prince. This feeling of a new Prince Album release would not leave me at all over the next 30 years. In the case of ATWIAD it was going into a record shop and picking out the vinyl (always making sure to select a pristine copy). In time vinyl would make way for CD's, but still I experienced the thrill of taking it home for a feverishly anticipated first listen. Further on I would find myself downloading tracks in the middle of the night. I was always excited to hear a new Prince Album release.

***

By now, I was a fully-fledged 'Prince fan' at the age of 13. What exactly was it that drew me to him? What led him to choose me as a person he wanted as a follower? Of course, the initial pop hits and subsequent albums were the manifestation of his work, his craft and his magic. But him? I didn't really know a lot about him, but that was part of the attraction and part of the mystery. He didn't do a great deal of press, so there wasn't a lot of him to pick up from. He may have made a film that was loosely based on his life, but this was a film - not 'him'. Being American represented an exoticism. America was the big land, the centre of the world and even if Minneapolis wasn't exactly renowned for much, it was still America. It was a world away from the West End of Newcastle upon Tyne, but noticeably similar in being situated in the North of the country and subject to harsh weather conditions.

Prince came from mixed race parentage which wasn't something I had ever come across. In the area I lived, it was literally black or white in the mid-80's and there was often friction between the two skin colours. I was part of the generation where it was becoming common for Asian children to be in the same class at school. I didn't see a problem with this, however others did. Prince would experience slightly more racial harmony. This was not without problems, but then Prince wasn't the sort of person who would frequent my physical world. He couldn't have gone to my school or lived in my street, and therein is perhaps a clue to the answer - dreams. Prince was clearly a dreamer, and very adept and articulating those dreams and visions through song and stage. I too have been a dreamer or a fantasist all of my life, from childhood ideals of space travel and sporting triumphs, to being captivated by music and music videos. These were all seeds that were being planted to push my supposed boundaries and challenge myself to rise from the, at times, harsh world in which I lived. I didn't experience an unhappy childhood - far from it, but I did find it sometimes difficult to be around people, more so as a teenager. Prince arrived just as I was about to become a teenager, and I got it - I got him as well as his world. It may have been all false, and I'm sure there was an exaggeration of a 'rock star' persona at times, but there was a bigger, wider scope than hackneyed gesticulations. Prince had a message - many messages. A lot of people didn't see the full picture or didn't want to with Prince. Some maybe got the 'hits' but little else. I felt as if I was taking my first steps into an uncharted adventure and I was on board for the full ride from the inception.

'Try my new funk'

During the period between the release of ATWIAD and Prince's next album 'Parade' I was afforded the opportunity to familiarise myself with and explore his back catalogue. This in the main, came in the format of copied tapes of his previous releases 'Controversy' and '1999'. Both of these albums were released before 'Purple Rain' and both were bought by my friend Darran or were bought for him as birthday presents. Each album was striking individually, but collectively delivered more angles and layers to Prince and his sound.

In '1999', which was at that point Prince's first double album, I could feel that he was at ease using the four sides of vinyl (copied onto tape) to the maximum to fully develop songs and expand on creating tracks for the dance floor friendly 12-inch single. Many of 1999's tunes are over six minutes long, yet they don't feel as if they outstay their welcome. D.M.S.R for example, just wouldn't work if it was compressed into three minutes. Its sleazy/sexy synths need to be drawn out and prolonged with the instrumental sections being just as strong and fundamental to the track as the vocal. This album was testament to the eight minute pop/dance song. It only has 11 tracks, but it doesn't suffer for it. This album is very definitely Prince arriving on the big scene. After a few years of near misses, he has hit on a brilliant formula and is ready to go even bigger next time. It's his album in waiting, and whilst I was too young at 10 to get it at all upon release in 1982 (I hadn't even heard of Prince at that point in my life) at 13, I absorbed it all. I may not have understood some of the more suggestive sides to Prince's lyrics/pronunciations, but I picked up enough in the music to dig the grooves and feel as if the music spoke to me, even it wasn't really clear what it was saying!

Whilst I was discovering Prince's funk/rock leanings (or 'frock' - possibly 'frunk'??), it was also very apparent that he possessed a much more tender side. The ballads I have previously mentioned ('The Beautiful Ones and 'Condition of the Heart') are – well, beautiful heartbreakers. I didn't know what heartbreak actually was then of course, but I kind of understood melancholy and Prince does melancholy very, very well. 'Another lonely Christmas', the B-side to 'I Would Die 4U' pours it out, as do both of the aforementioned tracks. So, already Prince has shown three or four sides to his writing and, with that, his personality. He would further develop this by adopting persona's or pseudonyms to produce or write for other artists, almost as if 'Prince' couldn't possibly say or do this, but 'Jamie Starr' or 'Christopher' could.

Jam 5 - 'Days of Wild'

Looking back to 1986 and the announcement of Prince's first UK concerts in five years, (his first large scale shows here), it didn't have much of an impact on me. It appeared unreachable, for many reasons. Finance was one. The ticket price alone was way out of my budget (unless there were some three quid tickets which offered a desirable view - thought not). Then there would be the location. London was five hours away from Newcastle via bus (the 'Clipper' was the popular coach medium of the time) and I wouldn't be able to get back after the concert, so I would need to stay in a hotel overnight. Both of these for a boy of 14 without parental accompaniment, were non-starters. There was also my perceived notion that he was untouchable; I could never actually see him live, in the flesh, could I? I hadn't yet been to a pop/rock concert and hadn't really thought it was possible at the age of 14.

Not many of my friends had been to concerts (Darran was the exception to this rule), so there wasn't much to compare experiences to, so ultimately it wasn't something that I spent too much time fretting over. It was great when Prince was in the UK as it coincided with the (limited) release of his second motion picture in cinemas 'Under the Cherry Moon' which I did go to see at the local Odeon picture house, even though I had to lie about my age to get in (and ironically lie about my age to get on the bus for 5p - half fare). It made sense that he would need to do some PR though. The reviews of the film, however, did not match those of the concerts and just as much as 'Around the World in a Day' was a very different album to 'Purple Rain', 'Under the Cherry Moon' couldn't have been a more different film to 'Purple Rain' if it tried!

Shot in black and white and only featuring Jerome Benton from the supporting cast of Purple Rain, the film saw Prince cast as a gigolo working in the French Riviera. Watching it on the big screen was an absolute thrill and I have to say I loved the film, even though I was very much in the minority. On the bus journey home, Darran and I enthusiastically discussed its merits and wowed over Prince's performance on our way to the chip shop. I still maintain the film, which admittedly does contain flaws, has a charm to it although I do appreciate I may be seeing this through 'Prince's goggles'.

Just two years after 'the summer of Purple Rain' (it wasn't really a summer of Purple Rain in the UK, as When Doves Cry didn't peak until August of that year, and I'm pretty sure the film didn't hit Number one in the box office charts, as it would do in the US), Prince was to play three live shows at Wembley Arena, London with his now fully expanded version of the Revolution, which now included a brass section and three male backing vocalists/dancers. In the period from first hearing 'When Doves Cry' and the time these dates were announced, I had listened to six Prince albums and had purchased most of them myself. I think the only ones that I didn't have at the time were Controversy and For You which I had on tape ahead of its full UK release. I had built up a small, but respectable collection of Prince related vinyl records (including a few 'limited editions'), had seen 'Purple Rain' on quite a few occasions and watched the television broadcast of one of the final shows of the 'Purple Rain' tour. Whilst this had been a heavily edited version of the concert, cut from a two hour show into a one hour broadcast, it certainly demonstrated that Prince was an electrifying and versatile performer.

Prince had also undergone at least two image changes and around this time gave an interview which was broadcast on MTV, while an edited version appeared on UK television. This was one of the first times I had heard 'Prince' speak on camera. He was 'The Kid' in Purple Rain and only said a few words at the BPI awards in 1985. This was much more candid, and saw Prince interviewed, whilst sitting in a group of what looked like extras from a video (he had shot the 'America' video earlier). Even now, this interview doesn't seem 100% natural and Prince appears guarded and nervous, although he does speak relatively openly. I loved hearing him talk in his soft voice and relay how he felt strongest in situations where he is surrounded by people he knows. I could and can completely relate to that and it is ironic that Prince is telling us this on camera whilst seeming somewhat tense surrounded by presumably (strangers). This gave me a great feeling of connection - Prince was clearly shy when being quizzed about himself, yet he certainly wasn't when he was singing or making music or performing. Here he exudes confidence and a large element of control over his surroundings. His band mates may not know what he is going to do next, although rumour has it that rehearsals for shows covered a multitude of potential set changes. I've never been a more confident person and to see someone I was already looking up to seem vulnerable and unsure of himself shocked me to some degree, but also gave me comfort.

'The Morning Papers'

The early collecting of my Prince fandom began to take an obsessive turn. The 'Record Collector' magazine became a wealth of information on releases not only from the UK, but around the world. Prince had, on average, to this point, released one album a year with at least two singles from each although the tracks promoted as singles would differ from country to country. Getting hold of the albums was relatively easy back then, but slightly expensive given I didn't start to receive anything other than pocket money until I was 18 where I started claiming unemployment benefit. Singles were harder to find, given their limited shelf life. Pre-1984, singles that had not, in the main, troubled the UK charts were deleted. Keeping up with new releases was achievable, although it did take frequent visits (at least twice a week) to record shops to ensure the latest single issued had not presented in a 'limited edition' run which was very much becoming the norm in the 80's. Picture discs, poster sleeves, double packs, coloured vinyl, 12-inch alternative versions, all appeared in the racks, but disappeared soon after.

Scanning through the article's in 'Record Collector' I was able to piece together the releases that had occurred whilst I was still listening to my 'Star Wars' albums. The singles from the

'1999' era provoked the most interest, as it became apparent there were not only a multitude of formats and re-releases with different covers, but also a sprinkling of non-album B-sides. Obtaining all of these particular versions of the singles would appear impossible - Where on earth could I get them? For a number of years, I had to content myself with merely getting what I could, when I could afford them, despite my compulsion to complete this wing of my collection. Eventually, in the late 90's/early 00's, Prince's stock would drop dramatically, and a lot of these previously seemingly unattainable releases were available at affordable prices, but in varying conditions. The advent of the Internet and eBay, Amazon and discogs now make it much easier to find, pretty much any release, as long as you have an unlimited amount of funds. Back in 1986, it was the record shops alone that were the providers. Some had mail order services which seemed a little bit of a risk and if I was going to part with my pocket money, I kinda wanted an instant return.

During a meander through an edition of 'Record Collector', I stumbled across an advert for a record shop in a part of Yorkshire called Otley. The shop was named 'The Revolution'. The logo was the same as that used on the Purple Rain album sleeve. There seemed little doubt that there was a Prince influence here and indeed the advert did mention Prince rarities and collectables. Talking this over with Darran, we were both intrigued and excited at the prospect of a Prince themed record shop in the UK and not too far away from Newcastle. As we saw the advert during the school summer holidays, I asked my dad if he would take us in his car to visit the shop, which he agrees to. I don't recall much conversation or negotiation needed about this and remain to this day quite surprised that my dad agreed so nonchalantly. It wasn't easy to get to and would mean he used a day of his summer holiday to do something he probably didn't want to do. Actually, I shouldn't have been surprised at all. This is the sort of thing my dad would do. He was a very modest man who always put his family first. Over the early years of my Prince fandom he regularly bank rolled requests for pocket money 'advances' or down right unreturnable loans. The fact that this money was often spent on a questionable product; I don't think the lyrics of 'Erotic City' or the 'Dirty Mind' album were really appropriate for a 13/14 year old, and my fascination with Prince's dress sense and style, provoked some odd comments, but nothing more.

Darran and I certainly had our eyes opened in a very beautiful way during our first visit to the 'Revolution' shop. We had already received a mail order catalogue ahead of our visit which was a few badly photocopied sheets, stapled together. However, it was enough to plot out our potential purchases. We found the shop. It was very small and modest, as a lot of independent record shops were, and still are. It used its limited floor space to fullest effect and we immediately became akin to the proverbial 'kids in a sweet shop'. My dad, very politely made himself scarce acknowledging that this was 'our world' and one we needed to inhabit unchaperoned - he would source an eatery for us. The record shop was Prince heaven. On display were countless Prince/associated artist items. A lot of these items we had never seen before and were imported. The 'Dance Mix' of 'Little Red Corvette' for example wasn't something we knew existed given that it hadn't been released in the UK. Needless to say, we both bought a copy (the last two in stock, as it turns out). I also went for a very fetching 12-inch US import of 'Purple Rain' in resplendent purple vinyl and a copy of the 'New Black funk' cover based German '1999'/'Let's Pretend We're Married' 12-inch. Darran got an interview picture disc and the 12-inch US version of 'Let's Pretend We're Married', which contained the studio version of 'Irresistible Bitch' which was as yet unheard by either of us.

Whilst in the shop, we strike up a conversation with the owner and proprietor Chris Dawson, who was extremely friendly and happy to chat about the shop, Prince, and the upcoming shows at Wembley, for which he had tickets. Chris was actually seen on the TVAM news report of the first night at the arena. In the background, on a TV monitor is the full length 'When Doves Cry' video which neither I nor Darran have seen at this point. We actually keep in close touch with Chris and visit the shop again a year later. After a number of telephone conversations, Chris unveils his 'side line' of bootleg tapes, which although illegal, we lap up. One compilation in particular sticks with me. It is titled 'From Now Till 1999' and contains not only some rare DJ mixes of Prince tracks, but also the rarest Prince track known at that time - the single only release 'Gotta Stop (Messin About)'. Again. This becomes the first time we hear this song, as well as the B-side to the original release of Little Red Corvette, 'Horny Toad'. It's fair to say that I played this tape a lot. It contained almost 90 minutes of Prince/associated artist's tracks, most of it new to my ears and a lot of the versions sounded extremely well mixed/sequenced.

This was my first (but certainly not my last) foray into bootleg material. I can appreciate that this area is not for everyone and I also understand from an artist's point of view it can surmount to loss of revenue. However, this was the 80's, bootlegging was rife, and it was all helping me build up my understanding of Prince. Whilst some of the DJ mixes were perhaps unnecessary, hearing tracks like 'Gotta Stop' and 'Horny Toad' and even the early versions of 'Just Another Sucker' were almost critical and, certainly, in the case of 'Gotta Stop' there didn't seem to be any other way to hear it, other than finding a copy with the help of 'Record Collector'. Obtaining tapes such as this were thirst quenching and very much filling a need. But I needed more. This set me off on visiting record fairs where I would find that collecting tapes and vinyl would become a very expensive hobby, and it still is!

Concurrently, I also first became aware of the 'Controversy' fanzine in 1986. Again, interest in Prince within the UK had gone up a few notches with the Wembley shows during August of that year. It was quite difficult to obtain 'official' information about Prince as it appeared that there wasn't a fan club or information service provided. Having a fan club was very much the done thing for pop acts in the 1970's/80's, so for a high profile act not to engage was slightly unusual. The only correspondence address offered on his record sleeves was via his record label. This would shift 360 degrees in later years as Prince became one of the first artists to offer 'fan subscription only' access to some of his recordings via the Internet, but before this, it was a very different game.

As per the interview he gave on MTV at the time of the 'America' single, Prince seemed quite guarded about what information about himself he wanted to be in the public domain and, from this point of view, it made sense that he wouldn't be sending out bi-monthly newsletters or annual Christmas cards (written by his manager and sent to a mailing list). This didn't mean demand wasn't there and one lady spearheaded the first UK publication devoted entirely to Prince and the Minneapolis sound. Eileen Murton was based in Croydon, originating from the North East of England and was a Prince fan. Eileen and her team produced the 'Controversy' fanzine which went from humble beginnings as a photocopied set of pages stapled together (rather like 'The Revolution shop catalogue) displaying nothing more than fan art images of Prince to get around copyright laws. This was a very wise move given Prince's feelings towards illegal use of his image. 'Controversy' would later become a full colour glossy publication which was ultimately produced with the cooperation of Prince and his people. A side-line saw 'Controversy' go on to publish a Prince book which went on sale in record store chains across the UK in 1990.

During the early issues, 'Controversy' was a mail order only publication and was advertised in the 'small ads' section of the music papers and through word of mouth. From what I know, Eileen had a full time job and 'Controversy' was her hobby project. What a hobby it turned into! 'Controversy' followed all of the rules, and ultimately it paid off - Prince co-operated and on one occasion provided a hand written translation of a set of seemingly undecipherable lyrics on notepaper headed 'Paisley Park...From the desk of Prince'.

It was very exciting to receive the bi-monthly copy of 'Controversy' in the post, most of which would come with a hand written note from Eileen. Eileen was always extremely friendly in her exchanges and happy to share information and experiences. I was lucky to meet her on a handful of occasions. She had genuine warmth and appeared very mild mannered and was not an egotistical person by any length.

As the Controversy network grew with Prince's UK popularity, fans were encouraged to correspond with each other, and I saw this as a very positive move. How cool would it be to create a Prince fan network and find like-minded fans in the North East? Other than Darran, I wasn't going to find any at school or at football matches which were my only social outlets during this time. I became very committed to finding fans and was lucky in that I did receive correspondence from a fan not too far away from Newcastle. We wrote frequently, about Prince and his music and eventually meetings with other fans were arranged. This was a magical finding; there were other Prince fans in the area! The group met semi regularly, initially in Newcastle, but later at houses and ultimately arranged to travel to London together in December 1987 to attend a Prince fan convention which was organised by Controversy fanzine.

I had never been to a 'party' like this before but wasn't going to let that fact put me off, nor the fact that I barely knew any of the other people travelling and the only thing we had in common was our love of Prince. This all gained momentum very quickly. It was, after all, only just over three years since I had bought 'When Doves Cry' and here I was going to London to a Prince convention/party. I was still only 15. My only hesitancy in concluding that this was a group of people who I felt ultimately comfortable with would be that, due largely to him having a newspaper round, Darran could not join me in this very social aspect of being a Prince fan. This was definitely an about turn for me, as I was extremely shy, not particularly good at meeting new people, and had experienced my first bout of depression earlier this year, following an assault. However, in the company of Prince fans, these self-imposed shackles seemed to loosen, and I could feel comfortable and a lot more at ease with myself.

This new found controlled confidence paid a huge part in me deciding on an outfit to wear for the party. My appearance would be crucial - I was going to turn heads. I could, after all meet a 16 year old Apollonia who would whisk me off to lake Minnetonka - not that I would know what to do if we got there of course. Whether my enthusiasm was transcending into something my parents could palpably recognise as a positive change in character, I don't know. But, in hindsight, it would be reasonable to conclude it did have a huge role in them agreeing to me attending the party, unaccompanied, and providing me with some 'spending money'. This was London, where the streets were paved with gold and the price of a drink (even a soft one) was comparable to gold bullion!

'High Fashion'

Part of my personal development as an adolescent was influenced by Prince seemingly being a different person, depending on mood/surroundings/company. I feel that I did, and still do to some degree, bounce off situations and react to how I feel on a daily basis. I could see this in Prince too; very much a good egg, but with it, a somewhat moody creative genius, perhaps uncomfortable in social situations where you are expected to be people's perceptions of yourself. I'm always uncomfortable in company where there may be unpredictable situations, or if I need to articulate myself. In my 20's and 30's, I got around this by drinking, quite heavily, often as a coping mechanism for my uncomfortableness in social situations, but in my later childhood years this was dogged with shyness and a lack of confidence. Prince 'simply' made great records and performed in front of thousands of thrilled fans. This was his coping mechanism. He became a different person on stage - a maestro, a star, a genius, and all at the dizzy height of 5 feet 2 inches.

Prince's height shouldn't be underestimated in my relationship with him. I come in around 5 feet 4 inches and have done so since I was about 15 years old. Being below average height had its merits but was probably outweighed by its perils. As much as I hate to admit it, it made me feel inadequate, threatened, and nervous. It made me very self-mocking, like I needed to over compensate and, at times, also be bullish. To this day I feel conscious about my height, especially given the usual struggles of weight and self-image. I don't feel that I carry weight well and am always looking to lose weight - at times, to the extreme. But back then, seeing Prince looking so god damn cool at 5 feet 2 and not only having the audacity to wear six-inch heels, but carry it well, just sealed the deal for me. It showed me that, no matter how negative I was about my height, the man who was fast becoming my hero had no such concerns. He walked, danced, played guitar, performed and courted, all wearing heels. His lack of height was not going to hold him back in any way. I would wear heeled boots at times to try and emulate Prince in this way, but they were far short of six-inch heels (although I will admit to 'loaning' a pair of my sister's black suede boots to complete a look I was going for).

I will be forever grateful and respectful of the dedication my dad displayed to me on what could really be described at the time as a 'teenage fad' from a parental point of view. I, however, knew otherwise. Not being a particularly communicative teenager (part shyness, part teenage angst) I could, and still can be, very sullen and prone to big mood swings. I don't and didn't often open up, but ask me about Prince (or football, which just about everybody in Newcastle has an opinion on) and I'm away. I switch personas and can talk without end on the subject. I was able to express feelings that I hadn't shown in my parent's eyes and became excited and articulate when discussing a new outfit or even the wild idea I once had that I'd like a spare room, made for me in my parent's loft, where I could house all of my Prince records and memorabilia. Inspired by the picture of Prince on the reverse of the UK 'Let' Go Crazy' 12-inch single, I would see myself lounging on a chaise lounge surrounded by flowers and Prince albums, listening to the latest vinyl from Paisley Park in my own world. I had this conversation (albeit on slightly more basic and practical terms) with my dad, and again he wasn't dismissive, although he possibly couldn't commit to it overnight. The idea passed (probably thankfully in my dad's eyes) and I didn't take it any further, but this did show me how supportive he was. Likewise, my mother, who did not dismiss my ideas of Prince costumes.

During the years 1987 - 1990, elements of Prince's dress sense began to creep into my wardrobe. Some were subtle, others less so. Buttons sewed down the sides of my jeans, as per the Purple Rain, Lovesexy outfits. Growing my hair, wearing a cross, attempting to sport a pencil moustache (unsuccessfully - almost as much as Prince's apparently was) were all efforts in gaining the 'Prince look'. If such a style existed. There was the flirtation with makeup (predominantly eyeliner), and the fascination with high-waisted trousers, partly coming from Morris Day, partly from the 'Alphabet Street' video). Polka dots became a fad in '88 and I wore a heart shaped badge on my wrist (as per the SOTT film). This went into overdrive on a couple of occasions and I had items of clothing tailored for me. Now, for someone in their mid-teens that is quite a statement but given that my mother was an exceptional seamstress it becomes more understandable.

It wasn't uncommon in the 1970's (or certainly in our family's social circle) for children to have clothes made for them which were usually knitwear and I can recall with great warmth (literally and emotionally) the jumpers, cardigans and tank tops my mam and grandma knitted for me. My mother (it's 'mam' in the North-East of England) worked as a sewing machinist until I and then my sister came along, where she subsequently turned her hand to looking after us. This again was the norm in working class England during the 1970's. The social revolution had not reached the suburbs and the male was the 'worker' and provider and the female was tasked (rightly or wrongly) with raising the family. This may sound very black and white, but I don't think it was a bad thing for myself and my sister. We were blessed with two very loving parents who worked hard at their roles in an aim to make life as good as they could for their children.

And so, how to link my mother's skills with a sewing machine back to an outfit of Prince's that would make me into the Bell of the ball!

Prince had already gone through several image changes in the three years I had followed him and always had a wide range of outfits on stage. However, these weren't the type of items that could easily be found on the rails of Top Shop, Burtons, or anywhere in Newcastle for that matter. For my exclusive look, I would need to talk to my personal tailor - my Mother! I don't recall the exact conversation, but it did all feel very natural to be discussing making clothes with my mam. She was a highly skilled seamstress and very adept at making clothes for both my sister and me. She had expertly fashioned a khaki suit for me in the style of Luke Skywalker in 'The Empire Strikes Back' when I was 8, so she clearly had form.

My initial thoughts were a lemon double breasted suit, as worn by Prince during the 'Parade' tour and visible on the cover of the UK issue of the 'Anotherloverholenyohead' single, and, as I would discover via the Revolution shop, the Parade world tour programme. This suit oozed class - glamorous, bold, and was both masculine and feminine. It was lemon coloured, after all. Contemplation complete, I think I concluded that this just wasn't exclusive enough. It was, all told a fairly traditional style of suit, even if the colour wasn't. So, back to the drawing board, or pastoral easel, as it were. I needed an outfit I could carry, and one that it would be unlikely someone else would wear. The 'Kiss' jacket could be the one, but, given it was leather, would be hard to replicate. Then it came to me - in the Mountains video (and the sleeve of the single), Prince wore a cropped jacket, with flared arms and hipster trousers. The neck of the jacket resembled that of a clergyman's. I also had a wonderful black and white still of Prince in this outfit which I have framed in my bedroom. Between the record cover, the photograph and some freeze frame action on the video player, I was able to show my mother the outfit she was to receive a commission to tailor for me.

My mother needed minimal direction but did say she would need a pattern to base the cut of the jacket on. The outfit took shape at an incredible pace, and despite my fidgeting at the numerous fittings, my mother completed a pretty much identical jacket to Prince's. It was a perfect fit, as were the trousers which I wore as hipsters. I was not especially conscious at baring my midriff, despite still carrying some adolescent 'puppy fat' at various times during alterations. The finishing touch is provided by a wide brimmed 'matador' style hat. Again, my mother comes up trumps and finds this in a fancy-dress outfit shop in town. Thinking back now, it does make me feel quite humbled that my mother spent so much time and money on this. What is also quite amazing is that she didn't really blink an eye and just got on with it. It is to her immense credit that she had confidence in her ability to carry it off. The finished result is just how I imagined it, with the silver buttons (again, expertly sourced - ensuring the correct style/design was appropriated) placed exactly where they are on Prince's. We even 'loan' a silk pocket handkerchief from my dad's wardrobe and make a silver heart to go over the breast pocket of the jacket - detail is paramount.

I felt great travelling to the party in the suit that my mam had made for me. People are genuinely astounded that my mother has made this for me and I get a lot of positive comments. I soon forget about that though and take it upon myself to derive maximum enjoyment from the event. The music plays on and on, track after track from Prince and his associates. I dance a lot and feel in my element. There are a lot of other people there including our North East contingent. I meet Eileen Murton, and many other names from the Controversy team. I seem to recall I tried to buy alcohol, but was refused - quite right too, although I really didn't need anything to assist me in losing my inhibitions. I feel great in my outfit, but my do I wish I had worn some footwear that blends in more appropriately than my brown slip on 'fashion' shoes. Still, at 15, you can still make naive apparel choices! I still have the outfit today. It was customised further for future outings. I had a Parade style crop top vest made and also added some logos. I had further 'Prince outfits' made for a number of years, but nothing surpasses this - a perfect fit and a perfect likeness, made by a perfect mother. Unsurprisingly, it doesn't fit now, nor should it, although I may be tempted to wear it to do the shopping in!

The 'Mountains' outfit, tailored by Carol Bell (my mam!!) December 1987

Not quite Wembley Arena, but a fine 'Parade' outfit

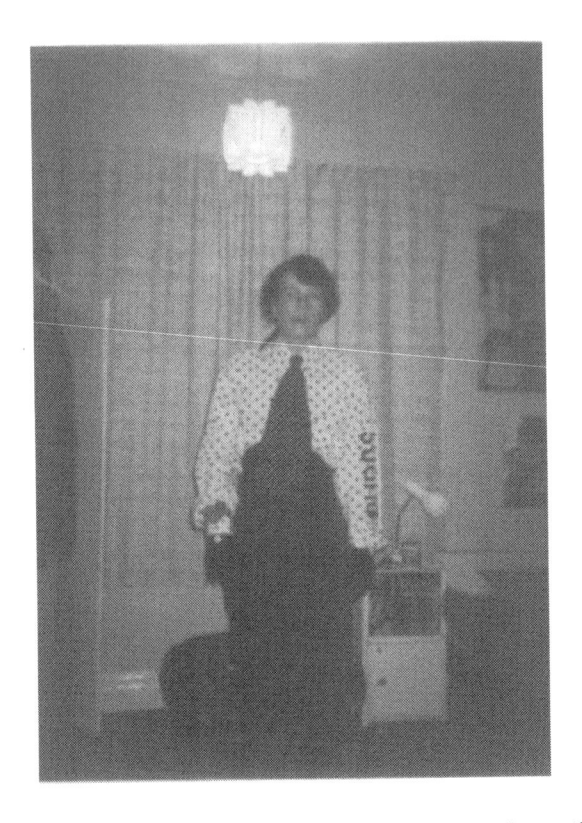

Not content with one creation, my mother also mastered another outfit for me, modelled during 1989 - predominately at a Prince fan party in Sheffield, although I did, on occasion wear elements of this outfit whilst purchasing Prince product in 1989.

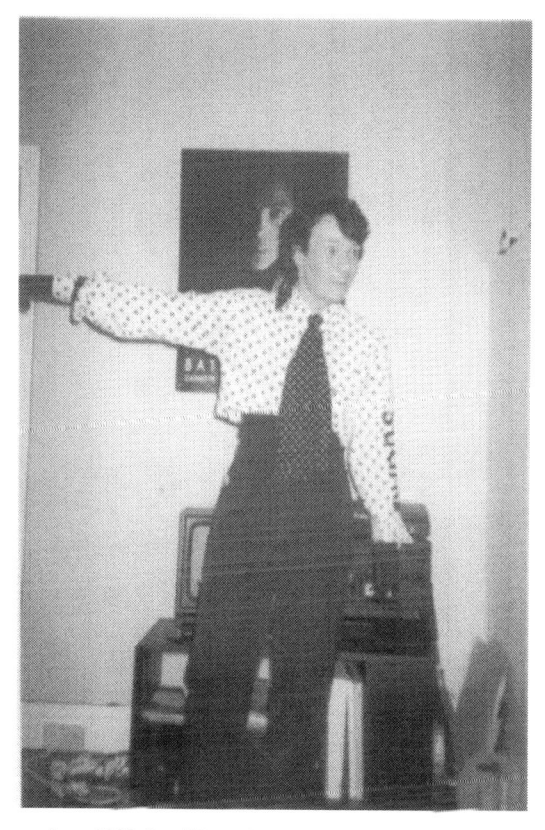

My bedroom, circa 1989, In all its princely glory! 'The latest fashion' indeed!

'My name is Geoff...or is it 'Prince'???? - difficult to tell us apart!

Jam 6 - 'Oh Yeah..'

Prince truly created sounds that had not been heard before and tackled subjects in a way no one had done in the past. For many (including me) this would peak with the release of 1987's double album 'Sign O the Times'. Released in March of that year, only 11 months after 'Parade', which itself was a year after 'Around the World in a Day', Sign O the Times was ambitious. Now without the Revolution, the release would have the feel of a more solo effort although there were collaborations and the Revolution do feature on the overdubbed concert track 'It's Gonna be a Beautiful Night'.

As was the way then, news of the album's release surfaced in the music press a couple of weeks ahead of the record hitting the shops. A few teasing titles were given, but I don't recall a full track listing being issued. The date was set for March 30th, 1987 - the date the most significant record in my life would be unveiled. Anticipation and excitement was building and increased during the weekend directly before it hit the shops when Radio 1's Saturday afternoon show, hosted by Johnny Walker, would play five tracks from the album as a preview. WOW! This was a definite 'tape to radio' moment, as most music fans brought up in the 1970's/80's will connect with. 'Taping' songs from the radio onto a cassette was a fairly common way to get music and save some money. However, you never got the full song, as inevitably (or perhaps intentionally) the DJ would talk over part of the track. For me this was very much an interim step to a full purchase of the track (that should cover the legal bit!!).

It was, to my mind, quite unprecedented for a radio show to feature so many songs from a new album. But this was Prince, and this was 'Sign O the Times'. The five tracks played were 'Play in the Sunshine', 'Housequake', 'Starfish and Coffee' 'I Could Never Take the Place of Your Man' and 'The Cross'. They were played in that order and not edited down, although perhaps 'ICNTTPOYM' was faded out. This was a rare treat and aside from the fact that I would be able to purchase the album only two days later, I was still getting palpitations at the thought of hearing so much new Prince music in one afternoon.

My memory tells me that I didn't quite manage to hear all five at home and that at least one track (possibly ICNTTPOYM) I listened to with Darran in his front room on his parent's stereo. This was the track, I think, Johnny Walker referred to as the 'Bruce Springsteen' track. I didn't understand the comparison - it sounded nothing like Bruce (who I was familiar with, but only on a 'hits' basis), but through time I can appreciate where the twinning of the sounds came from; 'ICNTTPOYM' does have that big, bold, guitar driven upbeat tempo that Bruce does so well. It also sounds great on the radio (in edited form - key for a U.S. hit) and has a story unfolding throughout the verses. Prince sings it 'straight' without voice manipulation and the song has the mass appeal of some of Springsteen's bit hitters. Perhaps this is the reason it becomes a seemingly appropriate lubricated singalong as observed by myself at one of the post Prince events I semi-attend. This was arguably as close to the pop/rock crossover of Purple Rain that Prince would present for some time, and that is no mean feat. In the scope of a double album, it is feasible to explore a whole manner of styles and influences, whilst pushing boundaries and creating new soundscapes. Whether Springsteen was an influence on this track, or in general it's difficult to say. I'm sure he would have entered Prince's stratosphere. They do cut very different figures (Bruce very much the white alpha male, you could have a beer with and talk sports - Prince the androgynous recluse who may not talk in public at all). But what cannot be ignored is their ongoing contribution to popular culture, music and live performing. The 80's were truly blessed with a batch of 'mega' recording artist/performers and solo artists in particular who all have longevity. The mid-eighties big hitters were Prince, Madonna, Michael Jackson and Bruce Springsteen, followed a little later by George Michael and, to a mildly lesser extent, Janet Jackson. This was a changing of the guard - these new stars seemed to take the mantle previously occupied by the likes of Rod Stewart, Elton John and David Bowie and, whilst each of these solo artists still represented big box office draws, the eighties were not their creative peaks. In fact, it is widely regarded that even the great pop shape shifting chameleon, David Bowie, suffered a nadir of output in the eighties, post 'Scary Monsters'. For me, all of them have a place in pop's rich tapestry and I have enjoyed, in varying degree, albums by each. I became, partly through the clear influence of some of the more 'arty' 90's 'Britpop' bands, a big David Bowie fan. This was helped in no short measure by an education from a close friend and first-hand Bowie expert, Mark Qureshi.

My wife is a big fan of Rod Stewart and once I stripped away the bombast and excess, I have appreciated a number of his albums and live performances. As much as I feel comfortable with the older guard of pop aristocracy, they were not of my time. Bowie aside, I couldn't get overly excited by a new album release from Rod, Elton, or Tina Turner - and let's not even discuss Phil Collins. All of these stars shifted big units in the 80's, largely due to 'Live Aid'. This not only helped raise awareness and funds for famine relief in Ethiopia, but also helped revamp careers of what can be termed as 'bankable' stadium acts. Prince didn't appear at Live Aid or contribute to the 'We are the World' single. Instead he did things on his own terms, shying away from the limelight and contributing a new track '4 the Tears in Your Eyes' to the USA for Africa album. The track is a gem. Understated and melodic with some great vocal harmonies from Wendy and Lisa. A very simple acoustic based song and yet another that could be added to the long list of 'wasted as a B-side' type outtakes.

I was now in the habit of trying to get records on the day of release, either after school (very possible to get a bus to town before the shops shut at 5pm) or, on occasion, during lunch break. This was generally saved for 'special occasions'. Thursday evenings and late-night shopping gave much more time to peruse and compare prices. The Monday visit would always be more focused on a one shop, one stop visit.

Obtaining 'Sign O the Times' on release day (March 30th, 1987) would not be without problems, and they were presented two-fold for me. As a double album, this would cost me more than I had previously spent on a record in my life. Even the 'rare' 12 inchers I had at this point, still came in at no more than £6. A newly released double album would be in the region of £8 - quite a jump from £5.49 for a chart album or £2.79 for a chart 12-inch single. Even the hip and well informed independent 'Hitsville' records that I was now a regular customer at, were guaranteed to sell most records at least one penny less than the high street, (with prices of '£1.98' or '£5.48'), would be selling the album for £7.98.

The Sign O the Times album release crept up and I was concerned. As I was absent from school at this period, due to ill health and both my parents were at work during the day. I had to find a solution to getting to the record shop (accompanied) on the Monday of its release. It absolutely had to be the Monday. The Tuesday or Thursday would not suffice. It also had to be the morning, so Darran was unable to assist on this occasion. This was the most important day of my life so far. My illness wasn't palpable, and it momentarily became insignificant in comparison to the thought of not getting the record on the day of release. I can't recall how I floated the notion that I had to have this album, and I can't think I would be so callous as to use the album's potential purchase as some sort of spiritual healing for my illness, but whatever I said or did, it worked, and I could not have been happier with the solution.

My Grandparents on my mother's side lived about a 30-minute walk away, or a ten-minute car journey. This was slightly further away than they were before we moved houses in the Autumn of 1983, but given that they were both relatively fit, the distance didn't preclude them from visiting us and on the period when I was not at school, coming to attend to me, for company, or supervision. I loved them both dearly and, given that I did not know my grandparents on my father's side, had nothing to compare them to and could pretty much see no bad in them. It seemed that every time my sister and I saw my grandparents they had a treat in store for us - sweets, pop, comics, or even simply the fact that we were seeing them, given the relationship between grandparents and grandchildren is very different than the one between parents and child. Grandparents are meant to spoil their grandchildren. It is part of the job description and mine certainly lived up to that! My grandma and I had a special bond, despite her initial disappointment that my mother had not given birth to her desired granddaughter at the first attempt! She often used to tell the tale, with a lot of humour and canniness that she had instructed the hospital staff to send me back when it was announced a baby boy had arrived into the fold. However, upon first seeing me and placing my hand in hers, there was a change of emotion.

My grandma, was a very warm, loving and kind person, occasionally frosty, but extremely generous. She had a somewhat care free attitude to money too. She lived within her means but wasn't afraid to spend on the best she could get in terms of food and clothing. She looked after her money, but also spent it well. Sadly, the same was not always the case with my grandad who had quite a gambling addiction to horse racing and would often (as was later explained by my grandma and my mother) take money from my grandma's purse to fund his latest bets. My grandma always blamed this for her lack of investment in property and, indeed she didn't own her own house, but lived together with my grandad, to the point he passed on when I was 16 in a series of council owned properties. There is no shame in this, but I do feel my grandma thought she had lost out on being able to hand something on to her daughter in terms of a house.

What she may have lacked in property, she more than made up for with love, and I certainly have more positive memories of than negative despite her stubbornness which became more of a factor in her latter years, along with the occasionally argumentative relationship she had with my mother. I could, generally see no wrong in my grandma and I think that was reciprocated, despite many scrapes. I loved spending time with her - she was fun, a raconteur, which sometimes meant she would tell the same stories she had told time and time again, but I would never tire of hearing her recite them. Sadly, she died in 2011, aged 91 after a short but painful illness, with my wife and I at her hospital bed side. I drew some comfort that I was with her to the end. She may not be here anymore, but my grandma does play a huge part in my Prince timeline, although I very much doubt it was significant to her.

It was, after all, my grandma who accompanied me into town on that Monday morning in March 1987 to permit me to purchase Sign O the Times. Thinking about it, this is a huge act of kindness and potentially one which I didn't appreciate at the time. My grandma would have no doubt walked from her house to ours and then got on a bus to town and back and then walked home, all just so her grandson, who wasn't technically supposed to be out and about at that time of day, could buy an album by an artist she would not have cared for, if indeed she had even heard of him. I have a vivid memory of walking up to the record shop on that morning, with my grandma, and upon her recognising the shop actually required negotiation of quite a few steep stairs to get to, she urged me to go in and get it myself while she waited outside. Now, whether the stairs were the whole story, or whether she was just being canny and acknowledged that this was almost akin to taking a child right into class at school and was now a path I needed to tread alone, is contentious. The romantic in me would want it very much to be the latter. My grandma had no interest in record shops and certainly not this one, which had 'modern' music blaring out of the open window and was populated by the young, a lot of whom smoked - as did the shop staff. To be fair though, the stairs were steep!

This was indeed my moment and once I left my grandma I went into a calm feverous/edgy state. What if they hadn't received the record? What if they'd sold out? I'd told my grandma we would only go to one shop as the nearest alternative was a bit of a walk away. What if it cost more than I thought? Would she help me out? What if the record release date, for whatever reason, had been changed?

Casually bounding into the shop, I thumbed my way through the 'new albums' section. I knew exactly where this was and if the Prince record had been released and was in stock, this is where it would be. I didn't know what the cover art looked like, but I kinda knew I would sense it as soon as it appeared... I was not mistaken. There was to be no doubt this was the album I was looking for. It had a large aqua coloured heart shaped sticker emblazoned across the shrink wrap with the title of the album and the information that this was a 'specially priced double album' ... Hmm not that special at £7.98, but this was to be a steal given the content. I rushed over to the counter and calmly asked for a copy of the album which was presented to me in exchange for the required remuneration. To my amazement and surprise, the carrier bag that I was given to protect the record on my journey home, was a clear one, with the same heart logo as featured on the album printed across it. WOW! I still have this bag, and whilst it is slightly musty, it remains intact, and houses the very same copy of the record, purchased on that day. I did, at times, have the bag (or a second one I got at a later juncture) on display in my bedroom window, although given that the room was at the back of the house we lived in, the desired impact was restricted to people in the bedroom, or the window cleaner.

Once the purchase was complete, I hurriedly returned to my grandma and we got the bus back to our house, eager to unwrap and unravel 'what Prince did next'. It does make me think that this was feted, that to some degree Prince had planned it this way - my favourite artist, releasing (what would be become) his best album, which would subsequently become my favourite album of all time, and putting my grandma, my favourite person, as my chaperone.

The cover art on the front of Sign O the Times gave a hint of what would be unearthed on the four sides of the record - busy and colourful on one half, dark and blurry on the other. Prince's image was only seen in half form, and he was apparently walking away from the stage set as his outline was right up front and out of focus - A blurring of his character, or a metaphor for him walking away from his recent past, to conquests and genre's new?

Prince had gone into creative overdrive. The album was originally proposed as a triple under the title 'Crystal Ball'. Unsurprisingly, Warner Brothers were not overly keen on the idea of a three-disc vinyl album so Prince, reluctantly, trimmed it down to four sides of prime, succulent Minneapolis acid - funk rock. The first fruits of this were the single and title track. Once again, Prince had come up with a new, distinctive sound that was completely askew to anything going on in music at the time. In fact, if you look at the lead singles alone from his albums '1999' to 'Sign O the Times', which span just five years, they cover an amazing scope of sound yet all feel like classic pop singles - from 1999 to When Doves Cry to Kiss to Sign O the Times (I've deliberately omitted singles released from 'Around the World in a Day' as the lead single differed across the globe). You would be hard pushed to find many similarities, aside from the fact that they are Prince singles and that they all have 'hit' stamped across them. It is almost as if Prince had deliberately written Top 10 singles every time subconsciously (or, indeed consciously, tuning into the minds of the radio stations and the record buying public). This may well have been the case, or perhaps Warner execs were just very good at spotting and releasing the most commercial mass appeal tracks from each record. In the UK, each of these singles made it into the Top 10 (although 1999 did require a re-release as a double A-side single with Little Red Corvette three years after its original issue). This run would continue, into the 90's, where Prince would have at least one Top 10 single each year for 11 consecutive years. Quite an achievement.

The track 'Sign O the Times' was released with minimal fanfare, echoing the sparse sound Prince presented with this track. Prince did not feature on the cover art, although many were tricked into believing it was Prince in drag, and not singer/dancer Cat Glover on the reverse image. There was no Prince in the promo video, which was merely images of the lyrics to the song, and there were few pictures of Prince released at this time. The single was almost anti-1999 - downbeat in rhythm and lyrical content. Where 1999 had urged the listener to cast away any fears of the apocalypse and party, Sign O the Times highlighted the plight of the mid-eighties world from an observational point of view. It offered no solution or exit strategy other than the hope of love and the optimism of child birth, with all of the responsibilities of bringing up a baby in the era depicted in the song. The listener most definitely was not being urged to 'party'. This song was pretty much as far removed from 1986's 'Kiss' as it could be within the confines of a pop single. Gone was the playful, flirty, coy, funk campness. This was replaced by a wistful yearning and sadness. Even Prince's voice seemed softer, less brash, but in keeping with the track. Lyrically the song is one of Prince's greatest. The machine gun fire rapidness with which he rattles off the lines could almost be rap, and the fitting of the words to the melody is poetry.

As with all 'new' Prince singles there is a non-album B-side track included, and this time we do get an insight into the less serious side of Prince. 'La,La,La He He Hee' is a love song of sorts and sees Prince compare himself to a dog, seeking a 'relationship' with a cat, vocally played by long-time collaborator Sheena Easton. This song (especially in the full length 12-inch version) has a much looser jam sound to it and does lend itself to Prince horsing around in the studio. The point being is that Prince horsing around in the recording studio is so much more interesting than just about any other artist of the time. It never ceases to amaze me how this track found its way onto the B-side of the single, whereas there appears to be a stack of outtakes that fit in more with the project. Perhaps this was all deliberate and Prince wanted something that couldn't be included on the album at all. Don't get me wrong, I like the song, but I like 'Rebirth of the Flesh' more!

The SOTT album would take more than one listen to fully absorb, digest and comprehend the 16 new songs prepared for this 2-vinyl disc set. I certainly knew right from the off that this was like nothing else I had heard from Prince or anybody else. Opening with the title track and single and moving on to the guitar driven rock/pop of 'Play In The Sunshine', it would be third track 'Housequake' that really caught my attention in the formal listening. This was one of the five that Johnny Walker had played, but the horn driven funk really jumped to life on vinyl. It comes in with the line 'shut up, already - damn' and a bang of a drum before the horns subtly take over, paired with some loose guitar riffs that aren't really riffs, but more like strums, while Prince, in a sped up high pitched voice tells us how to do the new dance the 'Housequake'. The vocal was a fuller use of the tool Prince had used on tracks '1999' and 'Temptation', but this time he actually sang in the voice rather than speaking one or two

48

sentences. It was Prince singing this song, wasn't it? The credits had the song listed as having lead vocals by 'Camille'. Actually, looking at some of the other songs, they too had Camille as the lead vocalist - What did this mean? They sounded like Prince, but just out of synch with his vocal pitch; enough of a change to make me question the origins of the voice, but also enough to really know it was Prince in some way. Actually, this would be one of the many strokes of genius within the album. Here was Prince manipulating his voice to create a female alter ego, thus enabling him to feel fully at ease with the feminine side of his personality.

It was no surprise that the more gender ambiguous tracks were taken on by 'Camille'. Prince wasn't so much pushing boundaries as discarding them all together. Certainly, in the case of 'If I was your Girlfriend' there are multiple layers to the track and the vocal adds an extra level of mystery and intrigue. Prince sings to his lover about the jealousy he feels towards the relationship the lover has with a best friend - the 'girlfriend' of the title being a friend who is a girl, as opposed to a girlfriend/boyfriend (or indeed girlfriend/girlfriend) relationship. Prince is telling the subject of the song 'I want to be your girlfriend' - I want to be closer than lovers can - as close as your best friend, and he proposes all of this in the Camille character. Prince perhaps feels that he, as Prince, cannot address this direct and sensitive subject, but as Camille, he can. This is perhaps over thinking the song, but it is quite a complex narrative. What makes this track so much more unique is that it is only a bass and drum machine used in the majority of the backing. Prince seems determined to show that he doesn't need to use the conventions of the guitar/bass/drum and moves to an emptier sound to fill the spaces. Less is more for sure. It was a hark back to 'When Doves Cry'. I was absolutely in love with the whole concept and empathised with Prince's ease towards his feminine side.

Always flirting with effeminate aspects to create his image, I became fascinated with Prince's sensitivity, more so given the beautiful women he was often linked to. There was never a question in my mind that Prince was gay (not that it would have mattered to me), but he was clearly at ease in female company - something that for large spells of my life I have not had a problem with. The only time this has come into doubt for me has been the workplace where I often feel uneasy in the company of a majority group of all women or all men. However, hand on heart, I have never had a job I have loved, so this may be somewhat irrelevant. I don't feel I've ever had a problem being friendly with females and I do put a lot of this down to Prince. Yes, a lot of his songs were about sex and there is more than an element of 'mistreating' or misrepresenting women in the purple world, however camp this is done. But there is also a lot of romance and a lot of beauty in songs and characters, and I felt a connection to this. Prince clearly lived in a different universe than I ever would, but he did leave a lot of messages and influences when he crossed over into my world.

Sign O the Times was a statement by Prince. He may have disbanded the Revolution, who many saw as the creative force behind his rise through Purple Rain to Parade, but here he was with a double album (trimmed down from a proposed triple) of the most original genre (and gender) defying music to date. He covered an awful lot of ground in the near 80 minutes and it, once again, sounded like nothing he had previously released. Some of the songs may sound unfinished, and contain quite harsh/basic production, but this traces back to an influence (maybe not an obvious one) from punk and paved the way for the 'bedroom producers' that became very much the norm in later years. Prince may have sat down with a four-track portable studio for the likes of 'It' or 'The Ballad of Dorothy Parker', but when the results are this good there is no need to over-elaborate with huge drum fills. It was almost an anti-80's 80's album, although in truth it is timeless. Nothing has dated to my ears, although a remastering would be a treat. The sound has never transferred particularly well on CD, and whilst the album has been repressed and re-released on vinyl (with subtle differences on the artwork), it would be pleasing to hear a truly 'digital' version. Unlike a lot of double albums, I don't feel there is any filler here, in fact, quite the opposite - I actually wanted more, and have devoured the bootleg tracks and released outtakes that are available from the period. I frequently go back to this album, but it has to be considered and planned as I need to hear it in its entirety - I can't dip in and out, play one side or skip tracks. It is a true work of art and requires that sort of attention, to be appreciated in full from the opening beat and 'Oh Yeah' of 'Sign O the Times' to the closing angelic harmonies on 'Adore'. I have so much to thank this album for and when I'm interviewed the day after Prince's death it is this album I reflect on most. Prince brought me so much joy and this album was the peak of his recordings. It came less than three years since I had fallen for my first Prince track, yet I would continue to be attracted to following him up to the day he died, some 29 years from the release of this record.

This album opened my eyes and ears and opened an awful lot of doors. In creating his new, fresh sound Prince would draw on a number of influences - some obvious, some less so, and over a number of years I have widened my musical tastes simply by attempting to trace the roots of the sound. As a white working-class male, I doubt I would have heard of, yet alone come to own albums by Sly and the Family Stone which is one of the more obvious influences of Prince's mixed gender and race backing bands. Or Stevie Wonder, who in 1984 was in full smaltz operating mode with the cheese fest 'I Just Called To Say I Love You' (which, incidentally was a big favourite of my dad's!!). The album is sprinkled with more than a moderate dose of James Brown. Indeed 'Housequake' represents very much a homage to the funk bank sound of the JB's of the 60's. Jimi Hendrix, Bob Dylan and Joni Mitchell all play a part, as well as the album having elements of jazz throughout. Not to mention an under-riding P-Funk feel which is perhaps less obvious. Clearly at 15 years of age, I had very little idea of any of these artists, James and Stevie aside, and they were only the basis of pop hits which were not quite the best representation of each. There was also a lot of genuine soul and more than a hint of gospel in the angelic 'Adore' which would, in time lead me to Marvin Gaye, Isaac Hayes and Mavis Staples and the Staples Singers. The line of continuum moves on and, again, I think it's fair to say that without Sign O the Times, or without Prince, my musical tastes and influences would have taken a completely different path. Without Prince, I question whether I would have appreciated (at various stages of my life) D'Angelo, Cody ChestnuTT, Laura Mvula, Leanne La Harves, Public Enemy and even hints and traces of Rufus Wainwright. I have so much that in my mind, maps back to this period of Prince's career and beyond. With Sign O the Times in particular, Prince displayed his musical magpie collectors skills, in a very similar way that David Bowie had done throughout the 70's - cherry picking the sounds that interested him and presenting them in a consumable fashion with a unique and original twist. Pop culture is blessed with innovators - music especially. If ever an album proved that Prince was one of these people, it was 'Sign O the Times'.

At the time of Sign O the Time's release I was actually off school and had been for a number of weeks. Although not mentioned at the time, this was clearly my first bout of depression. I lacked energy, withdrew even more from socialising around school and suffered mild agoraphobia. I simply did not want to leave the house without my parents. This was all brought on by a serious assault, followed up by two minor ones and some threats. Possibly not worth dwelling on this too much, but the events had a profound effect on me, and still do. Confidence is something I have not been blessed with, and these incidents did little to change that. The events are still extremely vivid, but then so are the acts of kindness my family and some of my friends bestowed upon me during this point. I will never forget Darran bringing me records and music magazines and other friends loaning video tapes. It would be some time before I (and probably more so my parents) would be comfortable with me going out unaccompanied and I would not return to school until just after the Easter break near the end of April that year, which saw the family take a trip to London for the weekend.

This was a huge adventure, but slightly overwhelming for me. I also imagine it came at quite a financial cost for my parents. This was my first ever trip to 'the big smoke' and if I'm honest, I didn't like it. London was too big, too busy, too loud and too frantic - nothing like Newcastle. When asked what I wanted to do one night by my dad I replied that I just wanted to stay in the room and watch TV. Probably not the answer he wanted to hear given we had come all this way at my request. I remember going to see the latest Sylvester Stallone film 'Over the Top' which is, to be fair, pretty poor, but it had a warmth about it that I can still see in the film today. We visited Madame Tussaud's and did some shopping. For me that meant the huge record megastores on Oxford Street. I may have felt lost, uncomfortable and, I guess, homesick, but show me a record shop and my face lit up - even more so when I found the Prince section and there, in all its glory was the 12-inch picture disc of 'Sign O the Times'. WOW! I had never seen this before and wasn't even aware of its release, but there it was. I swiftly asked for my wallet from my mother to see how much money I had left from the 'holiday money' my grandparents had given me (and also to my sister). I had enough and also enough to buy the 12-inch import of 'Let's Pretend We're Married' that Darran had purchased from the Revolution shop the previous summer - something that I'd not seen in shops in Newcastle. I also bought a large postcard drawing of Prince and an Arsenal football club hat (it seemed a bit 'exotic'). That was my money gone. It was likely around £15 in total, but it felt like a million dollars to me and I did get a sense of achievement that I had found a 'rare' Prince record in London. It made the whole trip special and worthwhile, despite my paranoia around the capital. Reflecting on the trip, as a whole, it just makes me appreciate even more what my parents did and, whilst at the time, I probably didn't thank them enough as I was in that stage of semi-rebellion juxtaposed with love for them both. I can't, in retrospect, thank them enough.

***

It is around a month after Prince's death that I have begun to listen to more of his music, but this is pretty staged and is not a random act. I'm working my way through some of his albums, but I am conscious that certain songs will be a challenge to hear. Naturally, I do this alone as it pretty much has been for a large portion of my music listening lifespan. I feel you can lose yourself in an album much more without company, although there is much to be said about the communal experience of enjoying music. Prince's music has always felt very personal to me with his ability to make an individual feel as if a song was composed purely for them. I'm sure fans of other artists feel the same way - That is the beauty of music and talent such as Prince's.

It is some way down the line that I choose to listen to Sign O the Times as part of my understanding of loss. Part of this is duty; the record listening group (Mr Drayton's Record Player) is to present 'Sign O the Times' as their tribute to Prince and have asked if I have a usable copy for the evening. However, I feel as if I need to listen to this album in full first as I have done on so many occasions, but now, I suspect, even though it will still be the same songs, it will feel different - and it does. Pulling the album from my collection (my Prince records are kept separate from the others), I think back to the day of purchase, to the first listen, to the times I have enjoyed this, to the time when Prince was the biggest thing in my life and how much I wanted to be like him, with his moody swagger and distant closeness. It's hard to say which was the biggest peak in my Prince fandom, but 1987 would be near the top of the pile.

The record is in pretty good condition - no visible marks on the cover (it is still in its shrink wrap, with title sticker), the inners are a little battle weary and I also still have a photocopy of handwritten lyrics to Sheila E's rap on 'It's Gonna Be A Beautiful Night', which was produced by the team at 'Controversy' fanzine. I am excited yet nervous to put the record on the turntable, concerned that it may well be scratched beyond audibility. This is not the case. The familiar drum pattern begins and then Prince's 'Oh Yeah' yelp to signal the start of the title track. Throughout the album, I experience a range of emotions. Naturally I reminisce, but I also feel very happy - this is an extraordinary album, and to my ears it sounds just as fresh, relevant and coherent as it did almost 30 years ago. Lots of the album genuinely warms my heart, sometimes at unsuspecting moments. The spoken section of 'The Ballad of Dorothy Parker', "do you wanna take a bath' - so nonchalant and throw away and yet SOOOO Prince in 1987. The image of the conversation taking place that actually had these words in it is real. He would say that, why would he not? And, it would make PERFECT sense. Visualisations of my imaginary mini film that never was to accompany 'Starfish and

Coffee' where Prince is walking through a technicoloured playground (Paisley?) with Cat, throwing out flowers and looking back at pictures of 'Cynthia Rose' - a sort of parallel world that I had imagined for Prince, came completely flooding back. The transformation of 'The Cross' from mellow acoustic softness to an all-out rock guitar assault and the anticipation of the point where the track turns on itself with an imaginary '2, 3, 4' or an 'ain't it the truth' as in the live film. I was awestruck by that song - Still am.

Approaching Side 3, Track 2, I feel my heart skip a beat and I my lip begins to quiver. 'If I Was Your Girlfriend' - the song I have put so much stock and faith in, actually makes me feel quite numb, almost frozen in a time when it pushed boundaries like no other song had and I understood every word of it...Well, almost. The cool beat, the manipulated vocals, the ton weight heavy, yet crisp bass line...'and we'll try and imagine...what it looks like...yes we'll try and imagine what silence looks like'...beauty...manifestation...Prince Rogers Nelson.

The album is ending with the heavenly 'Adore', when I suddenly remember - I think the record has a jump, or a scratch, or something, and sure enough there is a very noticeable click and skip in two places towards the end of the song - Oddly enough this doesn't spoil the record for me. It makes it feel more personal, as if it has been put there as some sort of insignia. No-one else will have a copy that jumps in exactly this spot. I don't want anything to spoil my enjoyment and sense of achievement at overcoming the self-imposed challenge of playing my favourite album back so soon after the artist's passing. It doesn't. It just makes me want to buy another copy. I'm a record label's dream!

Jam 7 'Rock n Roll Love Affair'

My fascination and the collectability of picture discs is purely down to their scarcity and aesthetic qualities. They rarely come with different track listings and tend not to play so well, but they do serve a purpose to look at. I always found it disappointing if the picture selected for the disc was merely a reproduction of the standard release single cover. Where Prince and picture discs are concerned, I have done exceptionally well in that I have, I think, a complete collection of all issued in the UK, the one US release and two later picture discs that were 'European'. Album-wise, in the UK, both 'Parade' and 'Batman' came with a picture disc edition, and there are also 'Lovesexy', 'Purple Rain' and 'Symbol' picture disc editions, although these are not 'official' releases and come under the 'accepted bootleg' category.

Picking a favourite is just as difficult as selecting a favourite track from an album, and, perhaps a tad decadent. These are, as I've mentioned, records with pictures instead of the regular black vinyl, but I like a bit of decadence so I'm going to go out on a limb and say the 1989 'Partyman' 12-inch is 'top of the pics' for me. The song isn't Prince's finest. There are better, and, arguably more commercial tracks on the 'Batman' album ('Trust' I always thought would have been a huge hit), but 'Partyman' does feature in the film and allows Prince to indulge in some characterising via the video playing his take on the Joker, the 'Partyman' of the song's title. The single came in a variety of formats; the now standard 7-inch, 12-inch, 3-inch CD single and cassette single (or 'cassingle' if you will) and I was now in the habit of getting all four upon release.

Partyman was followed up format wise with a second 12-inch remix - the 'Purple Party mix', which was interesting as it included snippets of previous Prince tracks slotted in throughout. This was certainly a frenzied time for Prince collectors as not only was the Batman period the most collectible period of Prince's career with each single in at least five formats and two reaching to eight, but also the first time limited edition remixes had been issued as a supplementary release. Remixing tracks was nothing new and the 12-inch single easily lent itself to experimentation and additional production of the 'radio' version of the release. Initially aimed at the dance floor or disco, the 12-inch remix became the norm for acts in the eighties with everyone from Cliff Richard to David Bowie having tracks presented in different formats for an 'alternative' audience. The reality actually being that it was no more than a marketing tool to tempt fans to buy essentially the same record, again to boost its chart position.

In general, up to this point, Prince (or Prince's record company) had sporadically introduced remixes of his tracks for 12-inch release. A lot of Prince's songs, in their original (or complete) form are long and exceed the radio friendly 3 minute preference, so they were edited down for a 7-inch release, which generally meant a rather lazy fade out after 3 minutes 30. The 12-inch however, could contain the full glory - '1999' for example contains an intro and ending in its six minute plus 'album' version and so was put out as the 12-inch single. Oddly, it is as far back as 1979 where the first non-album version of a Prince track is released on a 12-inch. 'Sexy Dancer' is a much longer, funkier, bass driven and groovier version and feels rife for the dance floor. However, it wouldn't be until 1985 that the next alternative non-album (and non-film) 'remix' was widely available. Of course, 'Little Red Corvette' had a 'dance mix' but this wasn't available on general release in the UK (import only, until the CD single was issued in 1989) and 'I Would Die 4U' in its ultra-long 10 minute plus extended version again, gained limited worldwide release status.

The 'special dance mix' of 'Let's Go Crazy' was in fact the version from the 'Purple Rain' film and so it would be that the 'Around the World in a Day' tracks would be the first time that a 'new version' of Prince's singles were available across the board and around the world (aptly). Single releases did still fluctuate in various countries, but both 'Raspberry Beret' and 'Pop Life' got outings in both the UK and US, although there were variations on the B-sides of both and the 'remix' was very different between countries for 'Pop Life'. Although not explicitly credited, Prince generally did all of the additional production on the extended or remix versions. In the case of the US 12-inch version of 'Pop Life' this deviated and was credited as the 'Sheila E Fresh Dance Mix'. No co-production credit outside of the Paisley stable was confirmed until 1987's involvement of Shep Pettibone with the alternative versions of 'Hot Thing' that was housed on the 12-inch single release of 'I Could Never Take the Place of Your Man'. This was very much a one off collaboration.

Many DJ's attempted to put their own stamp on Prince tracks, but without his official blessing. There are very audible and creative versions of 'Sign O the Times' and 'Baby, I'm A Star' amongst others, along with a vast amount of 'mega-mixes' of Prince/related tracks, some of which are put together with stunning accuracy for BPM compatibility. During the summer of 1988 when Prince was in the UK to tour the 'Lovesexy' show, he, so the story goes, met up with DJ and head of 'S-Express' enterprises Mark Moore. Moore was desirous to put his own stamp on some of Prince's tracks. This came to fruition when there was a second 12-inch for the 'Batdance' single in 1989 which included two Mark Moore remixes. These were certainly more Moore than Prince (if you pardon the pun) and followed the path that a lot of club versions at the time did, where there was perhaps only a framework of the original song and the producer added in more elements, so that it became a different track completely for a much different audience, in an attempt to push an artist to a wider population. Not that Prince really needed this, although it worked and further versions of 'The future' and 'Electric chair' were squeezed out in Europe for the Nude tour in 1990 as Prince had no new product to promote at that point.

The Batman period for Prince was very high profile, and, arguably saved his career, commercially at least. 1989 was due to be a 'rest year' following the completion of the theatrical, but, loss making 'Lovesexy' tour. However, a chart topping album and single (Batdance was Number 1 in the US) when he was allegedly only asked to contribute three or four songs to the project was a bonus. Released to coincide with the high profile summer blockbuster film 'Batman' directed by Tim Burton, Prince (and Warner's) did very, very well out of the releases. Prince would tour the album (in bits) in 1990, albeit with a much more stripped back show than the elaborate 'Sign O the Times' and 'Lovesexy' productions previously. Tapping into the collector's market from two angles, there were mass opportunities for multi-formatting the Prince singles. The only problem was that not many of them featured Prince. The general cover art were variations on the new Bat logo. Even the CD booklet for the album (and it was marketed as a Prince album) only contained one shot of him, looking more to promote the film with a series of stills from it. The 'Partyman' 12-inch picture disc was the exception. This depicted Prince in character form and demonstrated his commitment to this (and any) project he was involved in.

Prince created a character he would play in the spectacularly choreographed 'Batdance' video. Named after his star sign, Gemini was a split personality - half the Joker, half Batman - all Prince. A metamorphosis of the good and evil characters in the story, and, arguably of Prince's persona, 'Gemini' enabled Prince to play both the comic book hero and villain at the same time and carry if off like no other. For such a small role, Prince had clearly added more than he was required, or than was anticipated, in much the same way that he had completed a full album of 'songs inspired by' the film. Only three of which were ultimately utilised on screen. There are those that dismiss this short, but successful chapter in Prince's career, but I'm not one of them. He married commercial demand with a unique creative output, and whilst the album is not his best, it would not be his worst. There was something quite odd about the album, however, and it was something unique at the time. The album was the first time I actually took a dislike to a Prince song, and this did not sit well. 'The Arms of Orion' was just too sugary and not Prince at all, in my eyes. Darran agreed. This ballad was a duet with Sheena Easton whom Prince had worked so well with on 'U Got The Look' but 'Arms of Orion' to my ears was as far from 'slammin' as you could get. Prince had always had ballads or 'slow love jams' on his albums, but they never seemed to follow convention. 'Baby' as far back as 'For You' was a very innocent tale of unexpected pregnancy. 'Do Me, Baby' was funky and showed vulnerability - Prince's take on the soul balladeers of the time and songs such as 'The Beautiful Ones' 'Condition of the Heart', 'Sometimes it Snows in April' and 'Nothing Compares 2 U' were simply, heartbreakers. This was new ground in more ways than one. It was a sugary, syrupy, schmaltzy and to me, just not Prince. 'Scandalous' on the same album was much better, and the B-side of 'Arms of Orion', 'I Love U in Me' arguably bettered them both.

***

Hearing a song by Prince that I just plainly didn't like was novel and also begged me to ponder, 'is it ok to NOT like a Prince song'? Up until now I had put him as high up on a pedestal as possible and could see no bad in his output. It was a question I struggled with a bit, but ultimately concluded that no-one could have a perfect track record and that hearing a bad song made me realise that Prince was human after all. It was actually good to recognise that he could release the odd duff song. There were a few more across his career, yet I have never disliked a complete Prince album - It simply isn't possible. 'Emancipation' may be overblown and simply too long. 'Diamonds and Pearls' is way too mainstream in too many places and the involvement of the 'Game Boyz' was, frankly, embarrassing. 'Plectrumelectrum' would have made a killer 5 or 6 track EP and even the 'New Power Generation' albums are quirky and show Prince in a different character setting.

The songs I'm not keen on are a mere fraction of what Prince released in his lifetime. Of course, I'm looking at this through rose (or purple) tinted glasses and can accept where some would say his output tailed off after his 80's heyday. This is often tainted by the name change fiasco in the mid 90's where Prince would 'kill off' the Prince persona, become referenced as 'The Artist' (or, somewhat unkindly, 'the ar*e-ist') in a battle with his record company. Just as Prince could never shake the 'Purple Rain' links and comparisons, so he would never be able to be referenced without some mention of 'symbol' or 'slave' or interviews where he wouldn't answer any questions directly. This is unfortunate but is very much the way the media works. The album Prince actually wanted to bring out during the low points in 1994 - 1995 was, in my view, one of his best and 'The Gold Experience' was his last major selling studio album for some time - coincidentally it was the last with Warner's until 2014.

Jam 8 – Collecting Records and Thursdays

For as long as I can remember, I have been a collector, or a hoarder, which is often used as a slightly more derisory term to describe 'collecting' . This began with superhero comics, which were bought once a week by my dad, then continued by my grandma. I moved on to Star Wars comics, collected by my mam from the local newsagent on a Thursday. Thursdays were my favourite day of the week throughout childhood, for numerous reasons - The aforementioned comic supply always seemed to happen on a Thursday, which would be replaced further down the line with music periodicals 'Smash Hits', 'Number 1' and 'Record Mirror'. My dad would come home at dinner (lunch) time from his job and we would have fish and chips. Thursday would be a day we would go down to 'town' (centre of Newcastle) with my mam, whilst on school holidays. This essential (my mam got her fresh fruit veg and meat from the indoor market) adventure normally meant some sweets or a toy for my sister and me, as a sort of 'pay off'.

'Top of the Pops' would also air on a Thursday evening, and it became a staple family favourite early on in our televisual scheduling. Possibly best of all, Thursdays would be the day of the week my grandma would visit. I can recall rushing out of primary school, which was just at the bottom of the street where we lived, to see her waiting for me and my sister at the gates (this was before we were trusted to go to school ourselves). My mind's eye paints a picture of her waiting with open arms, a warm smile and a shopping bag full of 'grandparently goodness'. Other times she would be in the house when we got home, and on occasion, when I was off school ill (normally following dental extraction), I recount looking out of the window from the living room eagerly trying to make out her figure in the distance as she walked up the street and waving frantically with anticipation when she was in view.

The love of Thursdays would continue into adolescence. It became the day when Darran and I would go into town after school to make our weekly record purchase. For me this had to be offset with rearranging the time I would see my grandma. As she continued to visit on a Thursday she began coming earlier, at dinner times, (when my sister and I would come home from school for lunch). Thursday's still have a big appeal now. It's nearly the weekend so just one day left at work and, latterly, it is the day of 'The Record Player' - the vinyl listening group I get so much enjoyment from. Lots of pleasure seems to evolve from Thursday's, but there has been sadness too - Thursday was the day of the week of funeral's for both my dad and my grandma - In the case of my grandma, this was quite deliberate - I wanted to say 'goodbye' to her on a Thursday. April 21st 2016 was a Thursday - the day Prince died.

The comics I would receive were never given away or binned - well, not for some years anyway. I read them all or had them read to me and then I would carefully pile them up in sequential order to store in my (then) shared bedroom. Sometimes I would remove the centre pages if they contained a poster and pin them to my bedroom wall (it would be sometime before comic book heroes would be replaced by footballers and ultimately pop stars as my wallpaper of choice). Generally, I would take care of the comics and not be tempted to draw on them or cut them up as some of my friends did. OCD in its most primitive form...

When 'Star Wars' became a fascination, there were a number of merchandising opportunities which was a very new angle in films. There had been products before, but not on this scale and not to the format of near 5-inch 'action figures'. This was a game changer and every big film that followed would have a series of these 'toys' and accompanying accessories. These were relatively affordable and highly desirable and, once I got one, I wanted them all - My first obsessive collection! The main characters were in my initial sweep (Han Solo HAD to be the first), but then the manufacturers began releasing figures of lesser players - droids that were on screen for seconds, background characters from crowd scenes. It seemed to go on and on and with the release of a second 'Star Wars' film, there were new versions of the same figures - different outfits, different weapons, and much further down the line, different poses.

I got as many as my parents could afford, and still have them, but some are a little battle weary as, after all, they were toys and I played with them, recreating scenes from the film and imagining new ones. There are one or two prized possessions that are still in original packaging, although it has never crossed my mind to sell. I came close to parting with one of my 'blue chip' possessions - Han Solo's spaceship the 'Millennium Falcon' - arguably my most coveted childhood toy (my record player wasn't really a 'toy'). I was stunned to receive it at Christmas 1980 and find that my figures could sit inside. It is still boxed and stored under a bed. I'm extremely happy I didn't part with it as I recall the person I was going to sell it to got cold feet...the force was with me! I still collect Star Wars figures in a casual way - new films have appeared, which brings new merchandise, and there is the resurrection and redesign of a lot of the older figures. The market for such figures has also evolved and the purchase of them is not exclusive to children. It is relatively acceptable (but does raise eyebrows in certain areas) for a man of my years (which is well beyond childhood) to continue to purchase and display such items.

Football stickers/cards and similar ones for films such as Star Wars were next. As with other childhood/childish pastimes, this has continued into adulthood. I achieved a childhood ambition in recent years when I purchased a whole box of stickers, which may seem extravagant and pretty stupid, but It kept me out of bother for a good while, despite a large number of swaps! It seemed very natural to progress into becoming a record collector. I had served my apprenticeship and was ready to invest in a more adult based hoarding hobby, but, in truth, I don't recall consciously announcing to myself or anyone else that this was my intention. It just happened, as these things do.

Not long before Prince passed away, it was announced that as part of a re-negotiated record deal when re-signing with Warner's, that all of Prince's back catalogue LP's with the label would be reissued on vinyl including the original artwork. Some of the Warner's albums had already undergone this treatment, which gave collectors the opportunity to own fresh pressings of albums that in some cases, had been played so often they come with an underscore of a fried breakfast being prepared ('Starfish and Coffee with your sausages and side order of ham, Mr. Prince??'). Obviously getting hold of copies of records you already have is the very antithesis of record collecting. It can confuse some. My wife (and she is not alone in this) does frequently ask if I've 'already got that one' when another copy of 'Purple Rain' arrives. I, in response, point out that I have many different versions of records with the same songs on.

The first Prince re-issue in this series comes out soon after his death - it is clearly too late for the schedules to be amended. 'For You' is in record shops days after, followed a week or so later by 'Prince'. I buy both. They have differences in the inner sleeve artwork, subtle, but they are there. I don't play them immediately, or at least for a while, but it felt wrong not to buy them. The re-release schedule goes a bit awry after this. The albums 'Dirty Mind' through 'Purple Rain' have all been re-issued in the past years, so it will be 'Around the World in a Day' (the first Prince album I owned) which would be next, although due to what I presume are problems with pressing up the releases schedule and supply and demand of Prince product, it is actually Parade that lands next with ATWIAD close behind. Next its 'Sign' in all its double album, heart stickered-fronted glory.

Of course, the notion of purchasing an album I already own on various formats could seem odd. This is pretty much exactly the same LP that I bought in 1987 and I'm assuming this one won't jump at the end of 'Adore'? The vinyl will be new, but it's unlikely this is a remaster, more so a repressing with newer, crisper more durable vinyl, but essentially the same. This is the reality of a record collector and the way that record companies operate. It's a vicious circle. A record company will look to gain maximum profit from a product, so 'limited edition, deluxe edition, remastered, new pressing and/or picture disc', etc. etc. are all terms the collector will acquiesce to. I am a collector. I am a collector of music memorabilia. I am a Prince fan. I collect Prince music memorabilia. Vinyl is the cornerstone of my collection. I am from the last generation of first wave vinyl junkies. The 7-inch, the 12-inch, the 10-inch, the picture disc, the coloured vinyl, the poster bag, the double pack - This is my world, this is my era. Vinyl as the prime medium had begun its somewhat rapid decline in the mid-to-late eighties and was ultimately replaced by the CD, although the formats did sit together on the shelves as comfortable bedfellows for an all too brief period. In time, this would be replaced with the MP3 download and then the 'stream'. Vinyl has made a rapid return to record shops (it fits!!) and has steadily grown in popularity. Record listening groups, exclusive releases, record store day, specialist vinyl shops, and let's be honest, a huge slice of nostalgia have all contributed.

For music lovers of my age, there is no better sound than when the needle of a record player clicks into the grooves on vinyl. My ears are tuned to the depth and expanse of vinyl - a wider sound when pressed perfectly, which does seem to be missing from the MP3. I am the type of consumer who will multi-format. I am a record label's dream customer who is happy to buy a vinyl album for the look, feel and sound, but is practical enough to know that the most convenient way to consume music is via an MP3 player, so a download or CD would be bought alongside. I don't require a lot of enticement, but some labels are crafty and will offer exclusive tracks to each format to maximise impact and chart placing upon release and also test their loyalty of the fan. No one forces me to buy the formats. I genuinely like to collect them. Most of my collection has been played at least once, but there are the odd one that still sits unopened, untouched and is just to look at.

I've not counted how many records/CDs I have, but it must be close to, if not more than 1000. I'd say around a third of these will be Prince or Prince related. It's not hard to build up a collection of Prince products. His released albums alone total 30 plus (not including the albums that were released as MP3's only). Then you have the compilations, the protégés, the albums he features on and the albums he has produced and written on. This is before even considering different pressings, variations on covers, limited editions and picture discs. Singles are a whole new ball game. I've mentioned that different countries often received exclusive single releases with alternate B-sides, picture sleeves and vinyl colourings. At last count I have the Purple Rain album on nine versions and I understand another is to follow with the release of a deluxe package that had received Prince's blessing and oversight. There are many more to add, some of which appeal, some of which don't. Availability is often key, as is a fluid bank balance.

Singles (or 45's) were where the collection could flourish - albums were relatively standard, but singles didn't have an endless shelf life, and unless the song was a chart hit, there were limited opportunities to obtain. Initially, 7-inches were not often in picture sleeves although this soon became a standard prerequisite. Once I got my head around the 12-inch format ('an album of two songs'???) they were next. Picture discs were always the fascination, especially shaped ones. These were rare (presumably due to the cost of producing them) and in very short runs with demand often outstripping supply. In most cases you needed to snap them up when you saw them, which wasn't always possible due to purchasing priorities elsewhere. There would, on occasion, be a kind hearted soul in a record shop who would 'keep one back' until you returned with the money and, indeed, I did establish a good relationship with one record shop in particular who accommodated most of the limited run releases that Prince produced in the late 80's/early 90's, and I didn't seem to have a problem in purchasing from them

Prince's shaped releases were generally the bigger selling singles and came at one per album; a shaped disc of Prince on his motorcycle for the single release of 'Purple Rain', the 'balloon boy' from the cover of 'Around the World in a Day' for the 'Paisley Park' single. Two from the 'Parade' album - 'Kiss' and 'Girls and Boys' and a signature 'symbol' for 'Sexy MF' A lot of other single releases carried a picture disc, mainly in twelve inch flavour, and to my knowledge, were mainly exclusive to the UK. There has only ever been one official single issued in the US that got 'picture disc' status. Although I don't carry a full itinerary of the worldwide releases, I am relatively au fait with what is available via Discogs and can only see that '1999/Little Red Corvette' got the picture disc treatment 7-inch style, stateside. This changed in 2017, when this release was given a limited global run via Record Store Day.

Post 1996, Prince went into release overdrive. Triple CD 'Emancipation' was followed just over a year later with a 4 CD set of 'unreleased tracks'. The official bootleg album 'Crystal Ball' as well as a single disc 'vault' compilation and an NPG album. This is the rate at which Prince wanted to release products and was what damaged the relationship with Warner's. It was becoming increasingly difficult to not only digest this rate of releases, but also to afford them!

Not many collectables were available and as Prince seemed to drop down the scale of popularity, so did the value of some of his records, which actually made purchasing them slightly easier and affordable. Record fairs, once the treasure trove of the serious (and seriously loaded) record collector, began to decline. The Internet was taking over and it was much more cost effective to sell from home than cart goods around the country for some dealers. Crowds at record fairs noticeably diminished and 'bootleg tapes' of concerts and unreleased material had pretty much vanished. CDs replaced them for a time, but now that file sharing torrents were taking off on the Internet, even this was under threat. The bootleggers were being outdone and whilst as a collector, there was some sympathy, I also took a view that this was how it was and the stall holders at record fairs had done very well out of me in the past (sometimes through unjustly inflating prices). Therefore, this was a form of payback. The best dealers would survive as they simply switched online and became creative. Others held 'fire sales' of Prince material as he was no longer flavour of the month. At one fair, I was able to pick up (in varying condition) the original UK 12-inch of 'Controversy' and the second release of 'Little Red Corvette', the double pack of 'When Doves Cry (with 'free' 1999 12-inch) and, best of all, the 'Paisley Park' picture disc - all at very decent prices. This felt like a major lottery win and at times like these, a 'poker face' is required when looking at the prices. No need to rouse suspicion that records are being sold below value - After all, they are priced as marked and there was also the possibility of chancing your arm and trying to get a reduction on a bulk buy.

I was lucky to be able to scoop up a number of rarities at this time whilst also picking up the ongoing releases despite these being, in the main, CD albums or CD singles. Picture discs and coloured vinyl (indeed vinyl itself) had more or less disappeared from the market. It would be some years until I went back and looked to complete my Prince vinyl album collection and since his passing prices of any of his records have soared. About a month after Prince's death, around the same time I was looking to help with putting together the 'Record Player' evening tribute to Prince, I decided that I would go into overdrive and attempt to obtain the (what I had thought) previously unobtainable items that were on my 'wish list'. I already had a more than substantial Prince/'Associated Artists' collection (helped in recent years by the Discogs/eBay and Amazon web sites) and it covered pretty much every era of Prince's career; 7-inch, 12-inch, albums, cassettes, CDs, bootlegs, picture discs and coloured vinyl. Promos, concert programmes, posters, books, t-shirts, magazines, badges, DVDs, videos, clothing and even a tambourine all featured. My friend and director of Record Player, Steve Drayton, even recorded a short film interview of me talking about the collection for potential inclusion on a BBC run website project. However, I could still see gaps. Gaps I wanted to fill. Gaps I felt I could fill - within reason. Setting myself a financial limit would be key and not overspending to the point where I could afford little else. My wife had no objections to this, it was my money and I would be spending what was left of my monthly wage after outgoings. With no children to support, I would again turn my focus back to record collecting and purchasing as many Prince products as I could. This would also serve as part of my return to listening to his music. If I bought a vinyl record, I would have to play it - at very least to check for jumps/scratches.

The Internet does make collecting much easier, but also removes some of the romanticism out of the process. There is nothing like finding an unexpected bargain in a charity shop whilst on a wet bank holiday trip or stumbling into an obscure looking second hand vinyl store whilst visiting foreign climates and finding 'buried treasure'. The purchase of records from the Internet can also be more of a gamble than a shop/store purchase - Will it turn up? Is it as described by the seller? (Not always the case). Is it really what you think you are buying? 95 per cent of the time there are few problems with transactions, they are, by and large under the safety of the web service provider's name, which comes with a level of guarantee. However, there is a different sort of thrill when your purchases arrive in the post. Fortunately, it has been rare that an item doesn't turn up or is not as described. I did take umbrage on one occasion when receiving a supposedly 'unplayed' copy of 'Sign O the Times' which had more scratches than a flea ridden mongrel!!!

Studying my collection, and attempting a chronological approach, I contemplated completing 'eras' first and going right back to the beginning - 'For You/'Prince' era. I was thinking about what I actually wanted against what was available. 'Do It All Night' was a curious one - apparently released as a single in the UK (it didn't chart) 'Sexuality' had a German release in a unique picture sleeve, whereas 'Pink Cashmere' was released in Europe, but not the UK. 'Damn U' and 'Insatiable' issued in the US (although the former was promo only, still with a unique picture sleeve). The cover of the record was the attraction in a lot of cases, especially if it were a country exclusive. A Spanish 7-inch of 'Glam Slam' had a picture sleeve (as opposed to the PVC version with title sticker, favoured elsewhere). 'Controversy' in France had an alternative shot on the cover. I went into overdrive. Any Prince record I didn't have, I wanted, as long as it didn't break the budget. Of course, there were some that remained 'off limits' - the original pressings of 'The Black Album' for example. In lots of cases the prices suddenly doubled. The vinyl of 'The Rainbow Children' for example seemed to jump from an 'expensive' £200 to nearly £400 overnight, which was way out of my league. It was also noticeable that bootlegs or 'fan releases' (same thing, really) were becoming more prevalent. Presumably as there was no artist to sue the backside off the perpetrators.

Vinyl pressings of the 'Hit n Run' albums (the last albums Prince would release in his lifetime) became available, although not released officially by Prince's label. The quality of these was decent, but it was clear they hadn't been mastered for vinyl in the same way that 'Art Official Age' had, which was a true revelation when heard in record form, as was 'Plectrumelectrum'. I could truly pick out sounds that just weren't audible on the MP3 or CD, which had an earlier release. Pressings of the radio concert broadcasts that were aired throughout Prince's career (official bootlegs) flooded the market, with some questionable packaging in some cases. I often think how hard is it to include a picture of the artist from the era of the concert? I made no distinction, I craved merchandise, as much as I could afford, as quickly as possible, as if in some way, I thought buying up these records would bring me closer to Prince. It wouldn't. Nothing could.

Of all the Prince records, I ever thought it possible to own, the non-album single 'Gotta Stop (Messin About)' has always represented the 'Holy Grail' for me. Being the only Prince single not to feature on a studio album, it was the rarest released track of his to hear, up to the point where it appeared on the third disc of 'The Hits/he B-sides' box set, released in 1993. An out-take from the 'Dirty Mind' sessions, it very much fits in with this period and could possibly have slotted onto the album as a side 2 opener. Parallels could be drawn with a medium paced version of 'Sister', perhaps. It is a longer track (not by too much though) and carries a much more 'radio friendly' lyric. More suggestive than downright dirty, although still quite rude, the track was released on two separate occasions in the UK. In the US, it would feature on the B-side to 'Let's Work', which made that release even more collectable (the 12-inch version of 'Let's Work' itself is a must for completests, more so in US format, as the band picture on the cover is one of the best of the era and once more, is exclusive to this release). The two releases of 'Gotta Stop' in the UK featured very different picture sleeves. The first, a somewhat provocative image of Prince in 'short shorts' and blazer, looking frisky. The second, a much softer shot of him, showing only his head and shoulders. Neither release was cheap in the current market and copies were not easy to come by. I had been lucky to obtain an almost mint condition of the 'shorts cover' 7-inch in 2014, which was beautifully packed and posted to me. I always like it when someone has taken the time to preserve a record and pack it securely when posting. The 12-inch versions just didn't seem to be available at an affordable price and this was one record (or one of the few records) I genuinely thought I would never own.

My wife has often asked about my most desirable record, and I always reluctantly cited 'Gotta Stop'. I say reluctantly as I never wanted her to (or anyone) pay the prices regularly linked with a copy. Now was different. Now I wanted the collection to be as complete as I could get it. Realistically, it will never be complete as there will always be something else to contemplate - another angle, or a new version of a track that has only just been unearthed. For now, I could smell vinyl treasure- or rather smell the virtuality of it via the Internet - A near perfect copy to boot although, disappointingly, it has a previous owner's name stamped on the label. I didn't think too much about purchasing, although did negotiate the price with the seller, which made it seem like much more of a result when I ultimately sealed the deal. An anxious wait for delivery, but finally, there it was! It felt like a major achievement to actually hold my own copy of this record; a record I had wanted for such a long time. But after a few days I started to look for the next gap in my collection - there are always more records to buy. Collecting never ceases, even when major conquests are achieved.

Japanese releases have long held a fascination. The versions from this country are presented in such a different way and seem to be curated by a group of audiophiles. For the 7-inch vinyl releases, the record is separate from the picture sleeve with the artwork being presented as an 'insert' rather that a record cover. There is also often a card component with lyrics or pictures, or more often promotional blurb from the record label or partners. All of this is packaged into a polythene sleeve for protection. This has been thought through to give the record and artwork the maximum opportunity to be preserved.

A selection of the collection (January 2016)

Prince releases always appeared to have a certain air about them, right from the cover art to the music itself. It did always seem comforting and precious to see the 'Paisley Park' logo on the sleeve and the centre label on records. It confirmed a mark of quality and, although not always advertised, Prince was omnipresent in a lot of these albums.

Collecting and consuming Prince's music (and records in particular) would, almost inevitably take you to what were loosely termed as the "Associated Artists'. I was (and continue to be) no exception. Often, somewhat harshly brushed off as mere 'Prince vehicles' there is an incredible body of work contained in a lot of these albums and whilst there are some where Prince's input is more obvious than others, I do view them as stand-alone efforts. In the main, they just happen to feature Prince. The period 1984 - 1987 was probably the peak for quality 'associated artists' work, but there were still some great projects beyond this. At its peak (in around 1987) it seemed like there was something new on a weekly basis, and this was at a period where Prince had released a double album, a sprinkling of non-album B-sides and had another 8-track effort pulled at the last minute by his own request. This is only the songs that were put forward for official release. The year saw albums by Sheila E, Jill Jones, Madhouse (two) and Taja Seville. The standard and variation of these albums was incredibly high, and it was enjoyable to hear each one and tune it to a different flavour of Paisley.

Admittedly, there was nothing absolutely left field and each album would loosely fit into Prince's own funk/jazz/pop/soul sub-genre. Prince would give part of himself to these albums, but also allow the artist to develop and stamp their own identity. Sheila E, whilst being the drummer in Prince's touring band of the time, brought out the track 'Koo Koo' which has an overriding feel of Paisley, but is most definitely a Sheila E track and it received some airplay. Sadly, in the UK, very little of the 'Associated Artists' material bothered the charts and often, the releases could be picked up in bargain bins. The Madhouse project was particularly fascinating. Prince took the horn section from the Parade era, led by the wonderful saxophonist Eric Leeds and developed and expanded the sound to a much more jazz/funk-based trip, but still with a vague pop sensibility.

The whole Madhouse thing was shrouded in mystery - no artist cover photographs and little information on the sleeve. Even the songs were just titled with numbers ('1' - ''8' for the first album '9 to 16' for the second - even the B-side was '6 and a half!). '6' was an incredible sound to my ears. It was Prince, but not as I knew it. No vocals or heavy guitar or Linn drum, but it just made me want to dance and gave me a very happy uplifting feeling. I had found this sound, and no one else (bar Darran) knew about it. Moments like this gave me a sense that Prince was guiding me onto pastures new in a musical trek. I think it's safe to say that Prince and the Madhouse albums would turn my ears to jazz, perhaps not instantaneously (I was, after all, only 15-years-old at the time of Madhouse and not exposed to jazz music in any great form), but I can trace jazz curiosity back to 'Madhouse' and Prince, who, at the time did have some jazz undercurrents in his sound, and his touring band. They regularly would include an instrumental section throughout the show which was more often than not a take on 'Now's The Time' by jazz great Charlie Parker. This is what Prince did - he collated his influences and mixed in his own new take on genres to simmer and come out with something that was unlike anything else at the time. It was an education in music and my ears loved every bit of it, just as much as my eyes loved seeing the record sleeves, and, if I could have done so, my taste buds would have devoured them!

Such a feast of music was on offer in this funk rich platter that every time I read about or saw a new release, I licked my lips with anticipation. Prince clearly surrounded himself with great talent and used his skills and knowledge to not only develop some of the artists, but also to absorb the influences they would bring. From an outsider's point of view, it could be an opinion that the 'Associated Artists' were Prince's latest plaything that he would pick up and ditch at will and wouldn't have amounted to anything without his sprinkling of magical purple stardust. I can see this as an observation, and it would be hard pushed to see a lot of the artists actually getting to record label status if 'Paisley Park' hadn't offered a deal. But to dismiss this vast array of output as 'Prince cast-off's' is being somewhat premature.

Admittedly, you probably need an appreciation of the Prince stratosphere to buy into the extended recording library that offers the artists mentioned, but, it does give a fuller reflection of where he was and the contribution he was making. Even if the albums that didn't really spawn a mass of UK hits between them (Taja Seville's 'Love is Contagious' being the only single to hit the Top 10, which wasn't a Prince release), there are many variations on theme's Prince was exploring, and his contributions with his Paisley family are extremely noteworthy. It felt as if Prince was a Svengali figure like Phil Spector or Berry Gordy, or perhaps a combination of the two, rolled into one with a dash of David Bowie and a sprinkle of George Clinton. Indeed, as I would later discover, the worlds of P-funk and Paisley Park were not disconnected, in a number of ways.

Prince used different pseudonyms for production and it was very much the case that a sound equated to a character, a persona, a level of Prince's psyche that he perhaps was not comfortable with using under his own name, so the alter ego came into play. Take the 'Purple Rain' film for example - Here the three main groups all have elements of Prince in them - the sassy ballsy and sexy 'Apollonia 6' - perhaps Prince's fantasy of how he liked his women (Susan Moonsie of the group and Vanity 6 previously, were in fact, romantically linked with Prince long term). Apollonia 6 certainly could be criticised for an OTT approach to women flaunting themselves, although I did think a lot their lyrics were smart and put men in their place, which given in a lot of the scenarios, the males in the songs were played to be men like in 'The Time' with their, at times, sexist language (although, again, I think a lot was tongue in cheek), that wasn't a bad thing. On the surface, both of these bands offered an alternative to Prince's band 'the Revolution' who were mixed gender and mixed race, and mixed their sound, using heavy rock-based guitars and drums, with more dance based rhythms which were then drenched in synthesisers. In fact, I often thought that the Revolution were a mashup of all of the three other bands in Purple Rain (include Dez Dickerson and the Modernaires).

Morris and Apollonia showed more classic takes on male and female characters; but mix the two together and you get a big portion of Prince (or 'The Kid') - perhaps it was planned this way, and perhaps that's what Prince was more comfortable with and why he put so much stock in pseudonyms. Parts of himself that he knew existed, but he wasn't able, or comfortable to show in the 'Prince' side of Prince. He had to hide them to some extent, under a different name. I like this way of thinking (even in theory) and can look to multi-facets of myself and be comfortable with different parts of my being at different times, though not all at once, and not always when surrounded by the same people. In some respects, it could be seen as 'crowd pleasing' or fitting in, but I do think you react to situations and bounce off others. Prince clearly bounced off a lot of the situations he was in and was able to adapt and offer a part of himself to whatever he was working on - rarely would the very same part be utilised. Prince was able to bring out the best in others by bringing out the best in himself, and the songs and music that were created this way are quite astounding. More so, given the catalogue of diverse records he was releasing himself throughout this uber creativity.

Songs that were 'cover versions' and hits (with or without Prince's blessing) showed him as a supremely talented songwriter, if nothing else (and there was so much more 'else'). 'I Feel For You', 'Manic Monday' and the monumental 'Nothing Compares 2U' were all worldwide smash hits for other acts. In the case of 'Nothing Compares', this song, to me, always belongs where it was first released on 'The Family' album. Eric Leed's saxophone cuts through the track just at the point where you think it can't get any sadder. A tale of a crestfallen broken heart, the song begins with the immortal line 'it's been 7 hours and fifteen days since you took your love away' - even the unconventional way the exact timing is phrased fits with the confused malaise of heartbreak. In fact, although the song is a 'break up song' it is so deep and profound that the sorrow expressed is closer to actual grief.

The production on the original is astounding - starting with some synth meanderings, St Paul Peterson comes in with the opening line and is then joined by Susannah (Melvoin) for some gorgeous harmonies on the fills between the lines - an orchestra is introduced at just the right point and the strings compliment the vocals and enrich the sound of despair, perfectly. The absolute killer line of the song, comes in just after the sax solo and still, to this day, sends shivers down my spine - I have not heard a line with such sadness as 'all the flowers that you planted baby, in the backyard, all died when you went away' This is almost a metaphor for the death of the relationship, or actual death itself. I have incredibly strong recollections of reciting this line in defence of Prince when I have been involved in heated debate over his merits. How can this line be resisted or dismissed? It is pure poetry and utter genius. I can recall countless conversations with Darran (who actually bought the Family album and loaned it to me) over the beauty of the track. Like a lot of songs, the original is the best. I was never too keen on the performances Prince did as it seemed a bit too schmaltzy and 'big' - less is definitely more for this song.

It did feel extremely odd that the song got to Number 1 for Sinead O'Connor, who actually does a very good job of capturing the emotion of the lyric - as evidenced in the video where she sheds a tear or two. This was one of those occasions when I got very precious over a song - it was mine (ok, maybe Darran had some claim to it too). I found it, I loved it, and it was written by Prince, who, in 1990 was not being regarded quite as highly as he had been six years ago. Although still with quite a high profile, given the success of 'Batman'. And, later that year he would play to numerous fans in the UK as part of the 'Nude' tour (which was packaged as a 'greatest hits' show, and would include 'Nothing Compares 2U'), his hits weren't so big ('Batdance aside), he had cancelled concerts at short notice and appeared naked on the cover of his last album. He was, in the eyes of many, 'odd' and it did become at times difficult to defend him. With his 'gender bending' and high heel wearing, he was not the most masculine of pop stars. The Sinead O'Connor cover did win him a lot of respect, and, I'd imagine, some fans. This version was Number 1 on my 18th birthday which did (and still does) give me a very warm satisfying feeling. In all honesty, the song deserved to be heard by a wider audience. Ideally this should have been via the original version, which would have led to global success for 'The Family'...but maybe I wouldn't have liked that. This was one of 'my albums' and I didn't really want it to be shared - I was very precious about it, and although a lot of people would disagree (the members of the band for example) I was happy to know that only a handful of people knew of this record's existence.

'The Family' only has eight tracks, two of which are instrumental, but it is arguably the best of the albums of the Prince Protégés. The opening tracks of 'High Fashion', 'Mutiny' and 'Screams of Passion' gel so well together it's not hard to listen to them as a suite. The subtleties of Clare Fischer's strings, the tight, thudding rhythm of Jellybean's drumming that kicks into the second track alongside the complemented male/female harmonies of St Paul Peterson and Susannah glue the sound together. It all sounds so effortless, and the romantic in me would like to think it all came together in one take, with Prince working the board and directing the players to produce this gem of a record. Even the black and white cover art was a throwback to the matinee idols of the 20's and 30's - a tarnished glamour with lush pink undertones - there was certainly a feminine side to this kick ass funk!

The players in 'The Family' project were clearly talented individuals, which is also true of many of the artists Prince worked with. In fact, Prince seemed to surround himself with talent that he could absorb ideas and influences from and pass on his musical wisdom to. None more than Wendy and Lisa - the driving force of the Revolution and key players in developing Prince's musical palette, introducing aspects that he hadn't considered previously. There was clearly a creative spark between the three of them and the diversity in sound on the 'Around the World in a Day' and 'Parade' albums owes much to the band collective at the time, with Wendy and Lisa being omnipresent.' The three of them clearly had an intricate and collective work ethic and were able to springboard ideas between them, right in the middle of Prince's most successful commercial and critical career point.

I lapped up the cover of 'Rolling Stone' in 1986 which showed just the three of them together, looking relaxed and uber cool. Sadly, it wouldn't last, and Prince was destined to move on, or perhaps, set his band free. Upon the disbanding of The Revolution, it was no surprise that Wendy and Lisa worked as a duo (with input from family members on both sides) and produced three albums in quick succession from 1987 to 1990. The surprise was that there was no big hit single, with 'Satisfaction' being the only one to hit the Top 40 in the UK, and that only a minor hit (although it did warrant a Top of the Pops appearance in the Summer of 1989). As is sometimes the case, I actually thought this was their weakest single, with the power-pop of 'Waterfall', the upbeat 'Sideshow' and the much more funk based (and Prince sounding) 'Are You My Baby' and 'Lolly Lolly' all being superior in my ears. Wendy's vocal was certainly strong enough to carry the songs (Wendy had already proved herself vocally in taking the lead on such tracks as 'I Wonder U' and prominent harmonies on 'Mountains' and 'Anotherloverholenyohead') and the arrangements were structured as well as anything they had done with Prince. They were possibly not quite at his level as a standalone act, but, to be honest, who on earth was? It was very fitting that Wendy should take the lead vocal for the reformed Revolution who performed at First Avenue a few months following his passing. I have nothing but admiration for Wendy (and, of course I had a schoolboy crush on her - that sassy persona she portrayed in Purple Rain, coupled with her guitar playing and good looks were palpably appealing to a teenage boy), who really managed to hold together 'Sometimes it Snows in April' at these shows, with just her in the spotlight. It was very fitting and understandable the spoken line toward the end of the song was amended to be 'I often dream of heaven and I know that he is there' - I can't imagine there was a dry eye in the house.

Wendy and Lisa reconnected with Prince on the 'Planet Earth' album, released in 2007, for the title track - It was reassuring to hear the three of the them together on a new track, and my feelings were that none of the magic had been lost - they continued to complement each other, and it would be wonderful if more recordings of the trio surfaced from the vault.

If there was one track from the vast array of 'Associated Artists' tracks that any casual fan should be familiar with, in my view, it has to be 'A Love Bizarre'. Marketed as a Sheila E single and featuring on her 'Romance 1600' album, it is a duet between Sheila and Prince, and although he is largely uncredited, he certainly provides more than 'occasional backing vocals' This would arguably be Sheila's most recognisable song, although using a Prince heavy duet is perhaps a little unfair to her talent. Like Wendy and Lisa, Sheila produced three great albums in the 80's, before joining Prince's band on the drums for the 'Sign O the

Times' and 'Lovesexy' tours. This was a smart move by both parties and eased the blow of not having the powerful and loyal Bobby Z at the kit for the first time in Prince's career.

Whilst Wendy and Lisa were very much Prince's muses during the Revolution era Sheila was, to some degree, a female form of Prince. Both of similar height and stature, both very musically talented and both able to write killer hooks (although a lot of Sheila's first album was credited to the 'Starr Company', another Prince pseudonym). Another example of Prince writing songs in character or for different characters. 'The Glamorous Life' was a gem of a track about female aspiration - a sort of pre-Madonna 'Material Girl' story where the main focal character yearns for diamonds and furs before love. Not best suited to Prince's deeper vocal, Sheila pulls it off. A Love Bizarre, however, takes it to another level, and a different world. Here Sheila was operating in the same way Prince was - a new image and a new sound with each album. The 'Romance 1600' album was a bit darker than the poppier 'Glamorous Life' from 1985, but no less funk and percussion based. The song comes to absolute life on the longer 12-inch version and exceeds that on the near 13-minute album version, which becomes a wonderful jam.

Using the same technique of chords as 'She's Always In My Hair' which I can only describe as a form of driving synth strings, the lyrics are very dreamy, psychedelic and wistful; 'a strawberry mind, a body that's built for two, a kiss on the spine, we do things we never do'. Prince and Sheila don't sound uncomfortable singing these lines and there doesn't appear any awkwardness on the live version captured on the 'Romance 1600' concert video. Special guests for the show are credited as 'Prince and the Revolution'. 'Special guests' does not do the appearance justice at all. Prince, in particular steals the show. Sheila is no mean performer and she absolutely holds her own, but from the opening 'A, B, A, B, C, D' of 'A Love Bizarre' this gig now belongs to Prince. He exerts so much energy and swagger, whilst maintaining a sense of control, making it look so easy. It would be no surprise if Sheila and her band just sat back and watched - as stunned as the live audience and the many watching the video recording, which was released on 'home video'. I stumbled on it by accident, not knowing Prince featured and bought a second-hand copy from our 'Prince supplier' record shop in Newcastle for the sum of four pounds! As VHS became obsolete, so did this copy and it delighted me to get a version on DVD, transferred from a Japanese laserdisc a few years ago - The performance had lost none of its surprise and 'wow' factor.

Sheila became the public face of Prince's death; an erudite, articulate and relatable character, who was extremely close to Prince and was highly regarded in the fan world. The sadness and shock on her face as she briefly addressed reporters and fans outside of Paisley days after Prince's death was palpable. Sheila also performed a wonderful tribute to Prince at the Black Entertainment Television awards, which saw her and Mayte (Prince's first wife) hold one of his guitars skywards at the end of the set. How on earth Sheila managed to keep this performance together, given that it was only months after Prince's death, was beyond me, and more so, in the song and video for 'Girl Meets Boy'. Even though I have never met Sheila, and have only seen her perform once, it felt like she was able to put to words and music how I (and a whole lot more people across the world) were feeling. I felt as though Sheila was baring the grief of the Prince world, as well as her own. Sheila knew Prince better than most, and they remained in touch, despite their careers taking different directions. I'd like to think that in my notion of Sheila and Prince being equals and, to some degree, part of the same character, that part of Prince will forever live on with Sheila. It would certainly be appropriate if Sheila was involved in 'what happens next' to Prince's vault of unreleased material.

The 1987 releases from Prince and friends, just kept on coming! One of the greatest of the 'friends' releases came from an unexpected source. Jill Jones' first notable appearance was in the '1999' video - providing backing vocals alongside Lisa Coleman. Jill had a small role in 'Purple Rain' - playing 'Jill'. Other than as a backing vocalist, I hadn't appreciated that she was an accomplished singer and that such a low key, understated release would capture my imagination. Coming out in the summer of 87, there wasn't much to pre-empt the album, aside from the single 'Mia Bocca' ('my mouth' in Italian..(or maybe Spanish), I learned) which was released weeks earlier. I bought the single, without hearing it, which was becoming the norm for the Paisley Park releases - It almost didn't matter who it was that had a single out that week/month, as long as it was a Paisley, or a related release, I had to have it. My local record shop and soul/dance specialist recognised my enthusiasm for this particular brand and was eager to update me on new releases and/or any limited editions that may enhance my collection (and no doubt, the shop's profit margins) and 1987, in particular, seemed to have more than most years.

As it happens, I had actually heard part of 'Mia Bocca' before but hadn't really recognised it. Part of the string section and intro were used as incidental music in a scene from 'Under the Cherry Moon'. This was not an uncharacteristic move for Prince - he seemed to love playing games of 'cat and mouse' or 'hide and seek' with fans - tracks from previous eras materialising in different formats or on subsequent projects. 'Mia Bocca' had a great melody to it and continued the heavy brass section sound favoured by Prince at the time. The biggest surprise was Jill's voice - very strong, bold, sensual and feminine. There was certainly a playfulness to her persona, but it seemed a lot more focused than the slightly camp, fantasy characters of Vanity and Apollonia. Jill appeared to be more her own woman and whilst there were touches of Prince in the single, they were a lot more subtle. Jill's single sat perfectly alongside 'Koo Koo' by Sheila and '6' by Madhouse, both released in the same period. Perhaps the 12-inch version has not aged so well, given the prevalence of the 'high hat' effect, and it does stretch the song a little too much, but it is still a worthy addition and a good alternative version to the slightly more refined album and 7-inch version. When the album was released, I didn't expect too much, and upon looking at the track listing, I noticed there were only 8 tracks (9 if you include the intro).

That in itself wasn't such a negative as albums by The Time and Sheila were often low on track numbers, but high on quality. One title that stuck out from Jill was 'With You' - this song was a soft, tender ballad that Prince had included on his 'Prince' album in 1979 - A good enough song, but nothing outstanding when performed by Prince (he would eclipse it many times over), Jill's voice took the song to another level. The whole project has a large involvement of Prince, but is very much a solo album, as opposed to a band collective. On first listen, it was hard to pick out a favourite - the raw funk of 'G-spot' (a Prince out-take from the Purple rain era) - the bass driven 'Violet Blue' with its saucy breakdown to include squeezebox, or the up-tempo pop sound of 'My Man'. 'All Day, All Night' was another Prince out-take, and one he seemed to have held back for the right performer. Jill was very much it. It starts with a cool spoken intro, which raises to a scream on 'What Am I' and off we go on a nonstop ride with Jill in the driving seat and Prince very much an active passenger. Jill's deep vocal range is quite unique in the Prince world and works so well within the tracks of the album, ranging right through to the closing brass drenched 'Baby, You're A Trip' which brings the party right down to calm and ends the album just as it starts. This a very apt technique to employ - compelling the listening to flip the record and start it again.

In my somewhat biased eyes (and ears), there seemed to be radio hits a plenty on the record, but this was not to be the case. Whether the record was just 'lost' amongst the vast amount of releases from the Paisley Park label in 1987, or whether Warner's were just not interested in pushing the record and artist (I'm never really sure how the promotion of a record worked then, nowadays, artists (via the internet), can self-promote in a variety of ways). Three singles were released (although only one, to my knowledge in the UK), but, again neither troubled the charts, and, whilst I could muse about the choices of single (was 'G-Spot' ever going to get 'heavy rotation' on daytime radio??). There does come a point where it's just not going to happen. This does have a positive, or at least, it does in my eyes - Albums such as these become treasures, and develop a cult following. Very much like 'The Family', I only knew of one other person who had heard the album, for many years - Darran. In fact, if memory serves me well, Darran had a CD copy of the album, as he had the latest sound hardware tech well ahead of me. It's very noticeable that the Jill Jones album is extremely difficult to get hold of. With second hand copies of both vinyl and CD being offered on internet sites at a very high price. The album (at present) is also currently unavailable via streaming sites, so it would be hard for new fans or ones that missed the release in 87 (that in itself wasn't difficult) to hear it via legal means. It was with great joy and relief that I did manage to obtain a copy of the album that I could put onto my MP3 player, and experience the thrills of hearing it in a different light via a different medium, but, as ever, hearing it on vinyl remains, for me, the ultimate way to listen. It would have been interesting to know how Prince felt about this project, and indeed the many other he was involved in. Jill is still with us, and releasing albums, which sound very different from her debut, but are no less creative. Whether there are any plans to remaster her debut are at present unknown, but with the 30th year anniversary of its release imminent as I write, it would seem appropriate.

An angle of Prince's appeal was the ease with which he could apparently feel working with women - his productivity and willingness to share knowledge and collect, observe and transform ideas from a female perspective was fascinating. The tabloids would have a field day with each new studio partner and jump to the lazy (but not necessarily untrue) conclusion that Prince would be 'romantically' linked with any female collaborator. He may well have been. I'd prefer to think not, and like the idea of Prince combining ideas with his lady studio partners, but also offering them a different perspective through his unique vision and, to some degree, transforming them in some way to be a different or better person. I liked that he could count girls as friends, and not necessarily girlfriends, and then throw the whole thing on its head with the release of 'If I Was Your Girlfriend'...I always seem to come back to that.

Susan Rodgers was a name that featured on the sleeve notes of many a Prince project, although I confess, I had little idea to what an 'engineer' actually did. Susan, or Professor Rodgers, to give her full title gave one of the most informative and absorbing interviews regarding Prince (and music in general) I have ever heard in early January 2017 and spoke with such articulation and warmth, that I kinda felt I knew her at the end of the three-hour podcast. Clearly a very talented studio engineer, it was a revelation to hear how Prince was in the studio and her recollections of the lost classic ('Wally'), which Prince wiped from tape just after completing it and the way Prince would leave some of his band collaborators to add their part to a track with the words 'finish it', before he left them to it, without further direction. What was very apparent with Susan was that she was a fan first - before she worked with him - before she pretty much had to be on call 24-7 in case Prince suddenly felt the need to record - and he often did. It is very possible that the level of Susan's reminiscence may not have been aired had Prince not passed away as he was extremely secretive about a lot of what he did in the studio - hence 'the vault' in Paisley Park - a sealed unit where he locked away all the songs he had ever worked on. Susan's estimate was that for every song Prince released, at least another one was in the vault - that is astounding, given that Prince released near 40 studio albums in his career - many of them doubles.

Prince clearly had successful collaborations with a host of female stars, but also produced some great work with male musicians. The Time were the very first group to sit alongside Prince in the 'Minneapolis sound' - a sound, very much borne out of Prince. Again, the albums were credited to 'Starr' Productions, one of Prince's early pseudonyms, and were much more playful and less serious lyrically than Prince allowed himself to be on a lot of his recordings. You did feel a sense that Prince wanted to 'hang' with the Time, but they were perhaps too cool to let him.

Immaculately presented in suits and ties, the Time were not ones for flouncing about in ladies' undergarments on stage (they had Vanity 6 to fill that area), and were fronted by the cool, streetwise Morris Day, who had known Prince since high school. The Time albums released up to 'Purple Rain' only contained six tracks each, but they would be long dance/12-inch like versions of the up-tempo numbers, with a few ballads thrown in, although these were often over the top and contained a lot of spoken word play acting. The two tracks from the 'Ice Cream Castle' album which featured in the 'Purple Rain' film, were unbelievably camp but undeniably classic dance funk floor fillers. Every time I hear 'The Bird' I do just want to wave my arms as instructed by Morris Day - wherever I am! Prince allowed Morris the limelight in the Time, and as much as Morris was a charismatic individual, I often thought there were bits in each other's character that each wanted from the other. I could never see Prince being as brash as the on-stage Morris, or Morris being as shy as Prince often portrayed himself. In 'Purple Rain' I loved them both equally and differently. The horse play between the two bands ('The Revolution' and 'The Time') was genuinely funny - just like two groups of school children, and the performances captured on film are electric, vividly portraying the moment in time, the moment of Prince, the moment of the Minneapolis sound hitting the big time so, so expertly.

Purple Rain was, sadly, the last hurrah for The Time Version II (the first saw original members Terry Lee Lewis and Jimmy Jam fired by Prince for missing transport in winter conditions), although they would reform for the album 'Pandemonium' which featured in the sequel to 'Purple Rain' - 'Graffiti Bridge', six years later. Members of the Time would not remain idle, and with St Paul and Jellybean moving over to 'The Family' , Morris going solo and Monte Moir becoming an established producer, it left Jesse Johnson to have an extremely credible solo career, which, again, deserved greater commercial success - His 'Revue' album, and more so, his second 'Shockadelica' were a variation on the Minneapolis sound, with heavy guitars and synths over funk beats with a slightly more pop sensibility - certainly the case in the single 'Crazay' where Jesse duets with none other than Sly Stone to maximum effect. I loved it.

I could not write anything about Prince's music without mentioning Clare Fischer - a seemingly mythical figure (I had not appreciated until only a few years ago that Clare was a man), who Prince never actually met. Clare had his own orchestra, and the first recordings of the string arrangements crossing into pop or soul/funk would be with Rufus (of 'Rufus & Chaka Khan' fame). I understand it was Lisa Coleman who first introduced strings to Prince, and he would send tapes of songs for Clare to work on, the results being mailed back. The underscoring of Prince's tracks with this lush, full and yet subtle orchestration added a beautiful wistful undercurrent which was at its peak on the Around the World in a Day and Parade albums. Prince and Clare continued to collaborate, from a distance for many years until Clare's passing. Ever since hearing the touches of orchestra afforded by Clare onto Prince's tracks, I have had a love of string sections in pop songs. Prince wasn't the first to combine elements of classical music and pop, although he did it in such a way, with Clare Fischer's steady hand in conduction control, that you just might think he was.

I strongly maintain that just about every Prince album has its merits - From his 'Imperial Phase' in the mid-to-late 80's, through to the clutch of albums he released towards the end of his life (4 in just over a year), via the download only NPG music club efforts and even the two New Power Generation collections - there is at least one gem on each - more often than not, more than this. However, what did become slightly frustrating over the years was knowing and hearing some outstanding tracks via bootlegs, which were seemingly overlooked in place of, let us say less dramatic songs. Prince's death has opened up the issue of releasing tracks stored in his infamous 'vault' - a safe keeping place in Paisley Park where his unfinished/discarded songs are stored. Some of these tracks were teasingly released via websites and downloads, while some were available via less legal means. Most Prince obsessives will openly confess to hearing and, more guardedly owning such recordings - I am no different. Over the years the availability has fluctuated as much as the quality, and many was the time when I would have loved nothing more to hear finished 'clean' versions of 'Electric Intercourse', 'Possessed', 'Rebirth of the Flesh', 'The Rebels' album, 'Purple Music', as well as the original 'Empty Room' or 'Adonis and Bashea'. Now it seems, my wish will be granted, albeit by the cruellest twist of fate.

The music of Prince has taken me in so many directions and unlocked an unbelievable amount of music though the Associated Artists, and many non-associates, but influences. Prince's musical world became a labyrinth of creativity, with Prince holding a key to every door contained therein. I feel that was part of what he was about - not only pushing himself forward with his own releases but using his vast talent to unlock doors for a variety of acts, which may have never quite matched his own genius, but then, who realistically could (a notion echoed by Susan Rodgers). At the same time Prince was happy to take influence where he could and seemed to draw the very best out of the people he surrounded himself with, which could then be picked out, at will, for future use and expansion. Mapping Prince's sound has also afforded me an opportunity I may never have been offered had he not captured my attention. The world of soul/funk is not a one often frequented by white, working class boys from the North East of England, and whilst I would never attempt to lay claim to an encyclopaedic knowledge of the genre, a basic understanding, appreciation and thirst for the sounds was achieved by tracing Prince's roots back through music.

Jam 9 - 'One nite alone...Live/Wedding Feast'

Of all the levels on which I have come to love Prince, there is one, above all, which I will struggle to overcome the loss of for a long time. I have, to a degree, come back to his music and, whilst there is still a lot of emotion attached to almost all of his songs following his death (I still find 'Purple Rain' incredibly emotional to listen to), I can, at the very least, begin to see myself enjoying listening to his music again. This is best addressed when I am alone, where I can gauge my true feelings and dig deep into the meanings of the songs, on a personal level, and reminisce over how much joy they have brought to me, when Prince was alive. There isn't a reason I can't enjoy the songs again - They are the same songs, but the world has changed. The world now does not contain Prince. He will never be seen alive again. I will never see him again. This is where I struggle the most.

For any music fan, it is the peak of your aspiration to see your idol live, in concert. This is not as easy as it sounds, as many factors contribute. Artist availability, and willingness to tour (although, to contradict myself, many more artists 'hit the road' in the modern era), location, and, very often, cost. There is then the not inconsequential issue of actually obtaining tickets. This used to mean standing in a long line, mentally counting how many people were in front of you, but now, can typically mean a Friday morning off work, sitting in front of your computer, repeatedly pressing the 'refresh' key and then shifting instantaneously into a frenzy to type in credit card details against the clock. If you are lucky enough to have all of these in your favour, and obtain tickets for your desired performance (and often accompanying travel and accommodation), there are still the nervous waits for the tickets to arrive in the post (bluff old traditionalist that I am, my preference is still to have a physical ticket and not a crumpled print out from a PDF file), and then the wait until the day of the gig, which could be substantial, and subsequently throw up any number of scenarios that could prevent attendance.

I don't recall making a conscious decision that I wanted to see live acts/bands, it seemed to organically develop - I was always keen to watch concerts on TV and was lucky enough to obtain some VHS videos of various concerts/documentaries (or, 'rockumentaries', if you will) as Christmas presents in my teenage years (Duran Duran, Wham!, New Order and Madonna amongst them). This was very much a boom market in the early - mid-eighties, with the advent of the home video. Hours of fun guaranteed, and the opportunity, at the princely sum of around fifteen pounds (roughly the cost of three vinyl albums!) to own and watch at leisure (as long as your parents didn't mind) your favourite pop star in concert, or in promo video format, in the comfort of your front room. Concerts (or edited versions of the concert performance) were a semi-regular offering in the television schedule, obviously depending on what financial deal was brokered. Concert broadcasts took up a greater amount of air time post Live Aid in 1985. A notable, and pre-Live Aid broadcast was the edited 'Syracuse' concert by Prince and the Revolution, which aired in March 1985 - this was heavily condensed from the near two-hour concert, which was ultimately released as

'Prince and the Revolution - Live' later in 1985. This release, at £25 retail price, would be way out of reach, price wise. However, I was fortunate enough to find a near perfect second hand copy a year later (coincidentally in the same shop where I got the single album release of the 1999 album for 2.50!). The video came in two, hour long volumes, which had a fantastic group photo of Prince and his band on its inner sleeves. Having previously only seen an hour of the show, watching the full concert was a revelation, despite the somewhat off-putting lighting throughout large sections. This was Prince in his element - on stage, and was, I assumed, the closest I would get to seeing him. How wrong I would be proven to be.

The foundations of my concert going were laid when, at 14, my dad commented on me watching a TV broadcast recording of 'Queen:Live Magic'. I quite liked Queen though wasn't fanatical about them. They had played at Newcastle United's football ground in the summer of 1986, which had, by all accounts been a very memorable show. As I was watching the broadcast, late at night, in my bedroom (having, at that stage, progressed to owning my own colour portable television in said room), my dad came in and engaged in general chat. As a typical teenager, I was relatively unresponsive. My dad asked if I had wanted to go and see Queen in the summer, at St James' Park. I said I wasn't that bothered (although I now wish I had gone). To continue the thread, my dad went on to enquire if I was keen on going to something like that. Without really thinking, I replied that I would have loved to have seen Prince in the summer, but I didn't think he would let me go (this referring to the Parade shows at Wembley in August). He said I should have asked and that if I ever wanted to go to something similar, I should let him know. I have a sense that he was offering an olive branch, seeing that he was losing his son to the increasing distraction of pop music, which had replaced football and Star Wars as my most favourite thing ever. Football was something my dad and I watched together, but this had faded slightly over the past couple of years - I would go with my mates - it wasn't really the done thing to be seen at the match with your dad. This wouldn't last, and within a couple of years, I realised that it wasn't so bad and that I actually loved spending time with him.

Early in 1987 I went back to my dad with my first request to attend a live show. My favourite band, Duran Duran had announced the UK leg of their 'Strange Behaviour' world tour and would visit Queens Hall in Leeds. This was around 90 minutes away from Newcastle, but, as luck would have it, local concert venue (the City Hall) were running a coach and concert trip, which would seem an attractive and safe (ish) prospect. At this point in their career, Duran's star was slipping - two founder members had left and the last album they had released ('Notorious'), whilst projecting a much more sophisticated and polished sound had not charted as highly as previous releases. Personally, I loved the album - it may have been one or two tracks too long, but overall the funk base of the sound, with accompanying brass section really complimented Simon Le Bon's vocals and the songs. Nile Rodgers' production, as ever, was perfectly tuned to the pop ear and it was a disappointment that neither 'Notorious' nor follow up single 'Skin trade' (very Prince influenced) were not huge hits in the UK. Duran were very much a band of the video age and image was everything. Their videos were slick, they looked great in magazine shoots and their album sleeves had an art angle to them. Most of all, their songs had a huge appeal - wonderfully crafted obscure pop lyrics, which blended with meticulous rhythms and sweeping keyboards made them a perfect fit for chart domination, and became, quite literally, music to my ears. Hit after hit followed and each one seemed more mysterious than the last - this was music to take me to another world, very much as Prince's would do after them, and Adam Ant had done before. Duran fitted perfectly with my 'dream to dare' manifesto for my music - not that I had consciously created a musical manifesto at 11.

It was Darran (as with so many major events in my musical lifeline) who first alerted me to the Duran tour (a case of Darran Duran, perhaps??) and his eagerness to go was palpable. Darran was the only person I knew at this stage of my life who had been to concerts/gigs, having seen Adam and the Ants during the Prince Charming revue and Wham! On the 'Make it Big' tour in 1984 - I was quite in awe of this, and whilst there was no way I could have gone to either, I was very keen to experience the live band scenario. Queens Hall in Leeds was hardly Madison Square Gardens, but, for me it would open the gateway to begin some of the greatest experiences of my life and Duran was no exception.

As he had promised, my dad was happy to fund my trip, although there were some enquiries about chaperoning. I didn't question where or how he would foot the bill for this trip, but, in hindsight, I'm imagining that he and my mother made huge sacrifices, which completely humbles me. The fact that my parents would do this, just so their son could have an experience, which they would not be part of does bring out an emotion in me that makes me feel somewhat embarrassed at the sullen projection of large parts of my adolescence.

Being almost two years older than me, Darran covered the responsibility angle (even though he himself would not quite be 17), and, coupled with the fact that there was supervised coach travel to and from the gig, the deal was much more sellable. By giving his blessing, and monetary backing, my dad was, effectively signing off his son for a life on the road, well, as long as that road brought me back to Newcastle safe and sound!

So, there it was, Saturday April 25th, 1987, my first experience of a live band, and it would be Duran Duran. Just as they were the first single I ever bought, and the first album I bought with my own money, Duran played a primary role in my musical experience. I feel very proud of this, and, more so that this was my first 'gig' - Ok, so they weren't at the absolute peak of their powers, but they were still a big draw, and have remained a huge favourite of mine throughout their, admittedly roller coaster career.

April 25th came, and our journey was about to begin - physically and metaphorically. Aboard our transport we climbed. The coach trip down seemed to take forever, such was our anticipation. The vehicle appeared to be 80 per cent occupied by females, who all seemed a lot older than Darran and I, so we were clearly in the minority. Peppered with the combined aroma of highly powered perfume and alcohol, the coach was buoyant. Once we arrived in Leeds, many headed for the nearest tavern, whilst Darran and I took our place in the orderly, but expansive que awaiting the venue to open. Again, the wait appeared endless, and did attract some attention from touts trying to buy and sell any 'spares' - this all seemed slightly threatening, so I made sure I clutched onto my ticket, even tighter. Once we did get inside, it was a bit of a scramble as the venue was standing only, and, to be honest resembled a large gymnasium. Finding our feet, we were faced with a number of stalls selling various goods and merchandise. I was captivated by the merchandise stall, and still am to this day - Many is the time that I feel compelled to buy a T-shirt I won't wear, a programme I won't read, or a mug I won't drink from, but if the band logo is present, it becomes instantly desirable - no matter what the cost!

My first gig was to be no exception - in fact it was probably overkill. I hurriedly snapped up the tour programme, t-shirt, fold out postcard set and a huge poster, which was actually bigger than me and became a bit of a logistical nightmare during the band's set, as I had to place it in a carrier bag and position this between my legs, being ever mindful of the mounting masses around me that would surge, push and jostle in time with the music.

As much as Darran had prepared me for the experience of seeing a live show, I was still very taken aback by the volume of both the sound of the band and the screaming of the predominantly female crowd. I was very familiar with the Duran concert film 'Sing Blue Silver' which had scenes (some dramatised) of fans fainting. During the Leeds gig, there was a spell when I thought I might be one of them, so during one of the set's slower numbers, Darran, I and the posters had to move to the back of the arena, where I took on a bottle of lemonade.... Rock n roll, eh?

Seeing and hearing the band was quite a spectacular emotion, and I loved that race of adrenalin as the house lights went off and the intro sounded - It was very much enhanced by this replicating a heartbeat...and boom, stage lights up and there they were, straight into 'A View To A Kill'!! By the time the closing sing along to 'The Reflex' ended, I was exhausted. Overcome by the energy and temperature projected from the stage and the fans, it was quite a lot to absorb. A lot of ground was covered in the set, including nods to the recent off shoot projects Arcadia and the Power Station, and an impromptu 'me and my shadow' from birthday boy, drummer Steve Ferrone. Noticeable were the different arrangements in some tracks, with 'Save a Prayer' being played as an acoustic version. However, despite a number of potential showstoppers, I survived and more importantly, so did my poster! Amazingly, I was able to relive some of the show the next day as a repeat showing of the final Tube (a cult 80's music show) broadcast (coincidentally from Newcastle) was aired at lunch time, showing Duran as the last band to play a set on the legendary Tube stage - in exactly the same outfits they wore at Leeds!

It did take me a few days to get over the exhaustion/continued adrenalin I had post-gig and, indeed I even stayed off school on the Monday and paraded around the house in my tour t-shirt! This was it, I wanted to experience these thrills again and again and again, in the same, but different settings. It couldn't be with Duran, so Darran and I looked closer to home and the venue which had provided the coach and ticket package to Leeds - Newcastle City Hall. We had a couple of nonstarters, with shows by Level 42 (only one ticket available - we declined) and Terence Trent D'Arby (only seats right behind the mixer) not being the best fit. But then, out of the blue, and going completely against the 'home only' ethos, we received word that could change our lives (again!!!)...Prince was coming to the UK in June, playing Wembley Stadium as part of the 'Sign O the Times tour' - we HAD to go.

Despite our eagerness, we did acknowledge that attending this event was going to be a challenge. It was London, and on a weekday, so, for me, I'd need a 'get out of school, free' pass - although it was towards the end of the summer term and one day wouldn't hurt? Surprisingly (or perhaps not), both of our respective parents agreed, as, quite fortuitously, Newcastle City Hall were again offering a coach and ticket package. It would be a long day, and mean a return in the small hours of the morning, but this was not itself off putting - who needs sleep, when you are going to see Prince?

As plans unfolded, it was announced that 'Madhouse' would be the support, and the stage would resemble the chaotic fervent excitement of the album's cover. A new band was being formed, which included Eric Leeds (who would prove his versatility by doubling up with a Madhouse set and being part of Prince's band), dancer and model Cat Glover (she of the SOTT single cover) AND Sheila E on drums. So, this is how the post-Revolution begins??

Ticket packages from Newcastle City Hall (and Selby Coaches - the tour operators) went on sale via the City Hall box office at 10.00 on a Sunday morning. NOTHING opened on a Sunday in 1987 at that time, save for newsagents and car accessory stores, so this, in itself appeared odd. Little of any consequence would stop us and we arrived relatively early to queue. We had no idea how many tickets were available, however, more to the point, no one had any idea of the number being purchased by those ahead of us. Everyone seemed in good spirits, and, we got to the ticket office (which then was inside the doorway of the building) and made our booking. We were actually issued with our tickets for the show - Wembley Stadium tickets - with the twin towers in full silhouette form as part of the design. The fact that we were going to Wembley was not overlooked - this was the home of football, the national football team, the F.A. Cup final, the jewel at the centre of English football's crown. As avid Newcastle United supporters, we were both resigned to the fact that our team, would not make it to one of the 'showcase' finals in the near future, as they seemed destined to follow a pattern of relegation battles, and early F.A. Cup exists, so it therefore became easier to see Prince at Wembley - an American pop star - than our local football club!

Holding the tickets seemed like an achievement in themselves - we were going to see Prince!!!!! A mere two months on from the Duran gig, were going to surpass it - There was an emotion that life could not get better than this - Our fanaticism with Prince had grown very quickly in the two and a half years since 'When Doves Cry' and 'Purple Rain' in the late summer of 1984, as we attempted to keep pace with his change in direction and style...And now we had concert tickets! A quick once over of the ticket revealed that we may be quite a distance away from the stage and that we should 'wear something peach or black' - Prince's new colour scheme adorned on the inner sleeves of the album. No problem - black it would be! The shirt I would buy from Burton's at the bottom of Northumberland Street in Newcastle was of the canvas type that was very popular at the time - slightly oversized, with satin type epaulettes' worn with 'dress pants' - baggy, smart, US college style trousers - very much in the vain of chinos, which were also popular at the time, and, as I had a black pair, these would complete my look for Wembley. Slammin!

Excitement levels seemed to reach new highs on a daily level, as the countdown began. Suddenly we were at the week of the shows - incredible. I hadn't told many people at school that I was going to be off on the Friday and don't recall that there was a plausible plan in place. Returning after morning lessons from school on the Monday for 'home dinner', the thoughts of Friday were firmly at the front of my mind - I may be able to even get in a side of the SOTT album if I ate my dinner quickly. Just as an appetiser! During my food consumption, the telephone rang - I got up to answer it and found Darran to be the caller - not hugely unusual, but he sounded slightly down, and I was soon to discover why 'Geoff, it's Prince - he's cancelled Wembley' - To be honest, I thought he was joking, as we were renowned for 'prank calls' so I just laughed it off. Darran repeated what he said... This was either a very convincing prank of BAFTA award levels or he was telling the truth...which unfortunately, he was. Apparently Simon Bates had broken the news on Radio 1 that morning, which had now gained momentum and the rumour mill was in full effect - Poor ticket sales, potential inclement weather (this was an outdoor show in the middle of summer in England and there had been heavy rain in the preceding weeks... Really, who'd have predicted that, eh?), and poor suitability for the light show. To be honest, it didn't matter. It seemed our dreams were shattered. My mood was, at best, poor. There were some stories that Earls Court was looked at as a potential replacement venue - It was indoors and could accommodate...except the local council 'do gooders' wouldn't budge on their strict '4 weeks' notice to grant an appropriate licence for the event. And that was that. Not missing a trick, and eager to please some fans, Prince hastily scheduled in additional shows on the tour in Holland - No apparent issues with appropriate licences there, then? To taunt us, current 'youth show' 'Network 7' filed a report from the gig, that weekend, showing footage of the show...and some candid words from the ecstatic crowd... 'Well, you've got Wimbledon, we've got Prince' went one not so charitable concert goer. I was equally uncharitable with a foot cleaner I threw at Darran's television at that point when we watched the broadcast.

Further 'torture' was to follow - the music papers that week carried reviews of the shows, and 'Melody Maker' had Prince on the cover - a still from one of the concerts. They were doused in praise for the set. Could they not have lied? During the week, desperate to seek some form of reliability in source material for the stories, I had contacted the owner of 'The Revolution' record shop, Chris Dawson. We had made some purchases from Chris since our visit the previous year and would return a little later in the summer this year (this was part of my Dad's attempt to reconcile my disappointment at the cancellation of the show - The other was his idea to take me to see David Bowie at Roker Park, Sunderland as part of his 'Glass Spider' tour. It would be years before I actually appreciated what a thoughtful gesture this was, and I do regret my churlishness in turning down the offer). During the conversations with Chris, he let slip that he had some live LP's from the tour for sale, which were very limited and available for 20 quid. No questions asked of course. No questions were forthcoming, other than 'how quickly can I get one?' It arrived on the day we would have been going to Wembley and I took it round to Darran's to listen to. This may have seemed masochistic, but it was actually quite rewarding, and we ended up just thinking bigger and better things were to come to us from Prince - There were, they did...and soon.

Prince attempted to make amends to his UK (and more so) his US fans who missed out on the Sign O the Times tour by producing a concert film for cinema release. This certainly gave us more than a flavour of the eclectic eccentric and electrifying performances we missed. It would be in fact, the following year when Prince announced his next tour, which, again, incorporated dates in the UK. Initially, five at Wembley Arena - an Indoor venue, (so no chance of climate interference). The show was announced as being presented 'in the round' - I wasn't really sure what this meant, but it was explained that the stage would feature in the middle of the arena and therefore, give a much better opportunity to view the performance. The tour would present (or 'promote' in record company speak) Prince's new album 'Lovesexy'. A mere 14 months after the release of 'Sign O the Times' and six months after the aborted 'Black Album' Prince was back - again with a new sound, and image, as displayed in the video for lead single and Top Ten hit 'Alphabet Street'. Prince bore more resemblance to the cover of his second album, with shoulder length hair styled away from his face, although the comparison ended there - The outfits he wore in the video were new and colourful and like nothing else around at that time - Prince appeared beyond fashion, creating his own look - even having his name printed down the side of his high-waisted trousers. Gone was the two-tone peach and black of the previous regime, and in were bright, vibrant eye-catching hues. The video seemed low budget, but playful - very much like the song, which had hints of rockabilly to it. Interspersed with scenes of Prince driving in a car and packed with cartoon letters in the background, it was possible to unveil a hidden message in the video, which was publicised through the 'Controversy' fanzine - You needed to be quick and handy with a 'pause' button on your VHS machine, but it was there. 'Don't buy the Black album, I'm sorry' - A plea to stay away from the numerous bootleg copies of the album that had flooded the market (perhaps driven by the profit losing record company?) And an apology The apology was borne out of the story that Prince had experienced an epiphany over the release of the album and decided it didn't represent where he was spiritually and decided to pull the release from his schedule. This then led to the affirmation of his beliefs and 'Lovesexy' was born.

Controversy was not far from the release of 'Lovesexy', as the cover art depicted a naked Prince seated in an orchid, with some strategic placing of limbs so as not to reveal which side Prince dressed on (or anything else). This was Prince offering his soul, as if re-born, and would (in bootleg poster form) be an image I would have on my bedroom wall in large print (note the careful avoidance of reference to Prince being well hung in my bedroom). I think this concerned my parents slightly, and later on there was some reference from my dad to me being gay. Certainly, there were no girlfriends of particular note at this point. I had flirtations with wearing makeup, I had grown my hair and wore earrings, and was fascinated by an effeminate looking man who was now naked on my wall. To be honest, it never crossed my mind, but, I could see where this may have been derived from. I actually thought there was no more heterosexual man on the earth than Prince, and whilst he was prone to camp, he always seemed to be linked with some stunning women. Not being a parent myself, I can see now that I was just being looked out for and there was never any question about me being loved by my parents, no matter what I was 'into'. (I remember different concerns being raised the time I got my head shaved and wore lace up ankle boots, but, although at that stage I was taken by the skinhead image, I was no closer to becoming the associated Neo Nazi, as I was to experimenting with my sexuality).

The Lovesexy album itself was another stunning effort - perhaps a bit more organic and natural than SOTT - There was certainly less drum machine and more strings, and there seemed more of a flow to the set with songs interlocked to give the impression of one long piece of music in different movements - This was taken further by the programming of the CD comprising of one continuous track, which frustrated DJ's no end. Packed full of references to God and new power soul, Prince was taking his first step to create a new learning, a new gospel, a new spirituality. This was not lost on me, more so as the record release date coincided with the day my Grandad died. This was the first time that death had entered my life in a big way, and, not surprisingly, I was upset. To hear Prince sing 'I Wish U Heaven' and (during the closing track on the album, 'Positivity'), about there being a 'hang up' in every man's life, 'a whirlwind designed to put you down' going on to say, 'it cuts like a knife and tries to get in you, this spooky electric sound. Give up if you want to and all is lost - Spooky electric will be your boss'. 'Spooky Electric' was Prince's term for the devil. What he was saying to me (obviously) was - bad things happen, but don't succumb to despair and darkness - Be positive. I couldn't see this immediately, but the message subliminally did get through. I am not the most positive of people at the best of times, but, here in one of my first experiences with real sadness, was Prince, singing personally to me and kind of saying everything would be alright.

Lovesexy was Prince's first UK number one as the album topped the charts a week after its release. Prince promised some surprises in the live gig for his UK fans and would make up for the disappointment of the cancellation of his Sign 'O' the Times' show. After issues with distribution, the Sign O the Times film would also be released in the cinema this year (1988). I would leave school this summer, which is a significant moment in anyone's life. However, this summer, I would remember forever as the second summer of Prince. My summer of Prince.

As the Wembley dates were announced, frantic phone calls were made, and, as long as there was enough interest, the North East wing of the 'Controversy' fan network would arrange travel, for those successful enough to obtain tickets. The concert tickets themselves, were also being handled by the 'Controversy' network, from a fan perspective, in that there were blocks of tickets reserved specifically for subscribers. These weren't guaranteed and there was a nervous wait to see if the tickets were delivered to applicants in the supplied stamped addressed envelope. Both Darran and I secured tickets, although we would not be seated together. This was unfortunate, but it was, we both concluded, a small price to pay. Unlike the previous year's issue from Wembley Stadium, the tickets appeared very generic and not especially eye catching. However, we had them, and, given the events of the previous year, we cautiously prepared for our first night with Prince, which would actually be his last at the arena on this run - August 3rd, 1988.

Relying on radio and music papers (and occasionally TV) for any reports of the tour had numerous advantages and a big part of me yearns for these days to return. No live social media, no posting of songs filmed via mobile cameras. It was classed as a major coup if there was a clip on a news feature from one of the pre-UK shows. In the case of the Lovesexy (or 'Livesexy' as they were dubbed in some quarters), this is what we got - A few seconds of Prince walking across the stage, wearing what looked like some sort of costume from 'Dick Whittington' - singing to Cat who was perched on a swing! A front cover of Melody maker carried a full spread on the previous weeks show in Paris - It appeared to run out of superlatives in describing the experience, all of which was music to our eager Paisley ears.

Prince's arrival in the UK was major news and was covered, almost on a daily basis by the tabloid press. Pictures of him in a three-quarter length coat with 'lovesexy' lettering down one of the sleeves adorned the front page of the red tops. Reviews of the shows themselves were heaped in praise. Prince seemed happy and very amicable towards fans and club goers at his 'after shows'. There was even a story of him doing an in store signing session in one of the larger record shops in London! This didn't appear within his usual shy character, but, perhaps more fitted with his clarity of vision post the 'Black Album'. Of course, he could also have been seeking redemption regarding the cancellation of the SOTT shows the previous year. He need not have worried. He was forgiven. We loved him.

Deciding what to wear for this first live experience with Prince was something I mused over for quite a while. This was an event, more than a gig or concert that I had been to previously (I had by now been to a handful of other gigs). This was London. This was Wembley. This was Prince. This required thought. I could liaise with my mother and have a new outfit made from scratch, although this would likely take a lot of time - More than we had, in all honesty. My mother and I had to abort plans of creating a peach silk costume based on the Sign O the Times 'jumpsuit' Prince wore during the 'Housequake' performance, as it would take too long to create - Christmas would seem more achievable for this and the proposed Controversy fan party (as per 1987). Sadly, this never happened as there didn't appear to be as much interest from a North East perspective. So, I never got there, and the costume was not made, despite the material being purchased.

I looked at the 'Mountains' ensemble I still had from the 1987 trip to London and felt this deserved a second airing. It still fitted me, and I have to say, it was pretty cool. I decided to have it updated with the '88 logo on the reverse (as per one of the coats Prince adorned during his London trip), and I also added a few homemade attachments, which, in hindsight, probably made the outfit look a bit tacky and OTT, but it was all done with good intentions. Fully in the zone, I went into overdrive and created a few banners for the coach we would travel in. 'This is not music, this is a trip...we're going down to Alphabet St' in full 'Sign O the Times' font went the message to be attached to the back window of the bus, along with a heart with 'Yeah Yeah YEAH' (lifted from 'Alphabet St' itself).

The day of the gig arrived - we were to meet at Newcastle Central Station around lunch time and the coach would pick us up. By this point Darren and I were at fever pitch with adrenalin. We had purchased a bootleg of one of the earlier Wembley shows, so were quite clued up on the set list (despite the ropey quality), which seemed to start with 'Housequake', and, chatting and swapping stories with other fans en route. It was clear the anticipation was shared by all. Not even the fact that Prince was to meet with some of the Controversy crew that afternoon (while we were in transit) could dampen our spirits. This was probably the closest I would come to meeting Prince, but I don't feel cheated. I'm not sure if it would have been a good idea, as it could have tainted my view of him. What if he wasn't what I expected (and chances are, this would have been the case) - What, other than 'thank you' would I have said? Would I have made a fool of myself? (Most probably). Besides, there would have the awkwardness. No, I think I can firmly say, I have no regrets about not meeting him, as good as a story as it might have been.

Arriving at Wembley, my first thoughts were how big it was - My only experience of stadiums had been the football grounds in the North East, and, as big as they were, Wembley eclipsed them, although, if I'm honest, it was a bit shabby looking. It was a beautiful mid summer's evening and there were countless congregations of fans sitting around waiting for the arena to open. We joined them, sitting on a grassy verge, manoeuvring, periodically around the perimeter - observing various outfits, and the gate to the area, where the sound and stage trucks were positioned. Many fans gathered around this area, in the optimistic hope of catching Prince's exciting sound check. Some had clearly been lucky, as we could make out some band signatures on clothing... 'Miko' and 'Levi' were readable - No Prince, that I could see.

Once inside the arena, my memory is of having cans of soft drinks taken off us, which seemed harsh. But rules are rules, and perhaps these ended up with Prince. Or, perhaps not. The inside of the arena didn't seem particularly glamorous, but then I'm not sure what my expectations were - It wasn't the era of glitz in the foyer - that was all saved for the show. Venues were functional and had been designed in some distant past where aesthetics and customer comfort were yet to be discovered - very much in line with the dated, and generally unsafe football stadia of the time. The arena, however was lit up with the omnipresent and inviting merchandise stalls...They needed to be patronised in abundance.

I had budgeted to cover a wide range of scenarios and wasn't disappointed. Pretty soon I had snapped up a T-shirt (in the style of the heart logo on the inner sleeve of the album which spelled 'Yes', fitting in with the song 'positivity') - I particularly liked the logo on the sleeve of the t-shirt (although my mother's washing machine didn't), three posters (Cat, Sheila and a band shot) and a tour programme. This had one of the campest pictures of Prince I have seen on the cover - full make up (including blusher and green eyeshadow) and an American policeman's hat, large earring and neck decoration and coupled with his pose, which wasn't exactly alpha male, it did look, at best, a bit silly. Still, I had to have it - the glossy, large colourful pictures that were displayed were just screaming to be devoured - for years to come. As with Duran Duran, the purchase of posters proved a problem - they weren't easy to store during the show and certainly there was no guarantee that they would remain unscathed throughout the duration of the show.

Entering into the actual arena alone (our tickets were dotted across the venue) - I found that my seat was actually in the floor area, where the stage was (as per the description, it was 'in the round' or in the middle). I spotted a few faces from 'Controversy' parties/gatherings - most notably Eileen Murton, the lady behind the fanzine. We chatted briefly, and she confirmed that she and a small group of fans had met Prince and the band that day, for a short period. 'What did he say' I asked - 'Not a lot' was her precise and, perhaps, slightly disappointed sounding response. I didn't want to know any more.

Returning to my seat, my heart seemed to go into overdrive until the house lights went down and what sounded like an amplified car engine started up. The noise filled the arena, as did the cheering and screaming. A drum beat to a 1, 2, 3 rhythms, then, just coming into sight, amid more screams was a full life size prototype of Prince's T-bird - just like the Alphabet Street video. The car circled the stage, stopped and raised up so the driver could climb out...'snare drum pound on the two and four...all the party get on the floor' - even typing it now, I can feel goosebumps rising - The first words I heard Prince speak live. And then, there he was - white polka dot suit, black cravat, hair tied with what resembled a large ribbon holding his hair in place. I was so transfixed by him that the music passed me by initially, until it registered that this was Erotic City - First stop on the trip of a lifetime. He prowled the stage, marking his ground, joined by Sheila and Cat..'All of my Purple life...I've been looking for a dame' 'woah woah woah...shuddup already damn' swiftly into 'Housequake'. The crowd, including myself, who had barely caught breath were grooving along with the kick ass tune until suddenly the tempo was brought right down with 'Slow Love' which saw Prince playfully serenading Cat.

The whole set up of the stage meant that you could quite easily see the interchanging of the band members - each one given their moment in the spotlight. A basketball hoop was in view - as well as a swing - this was most definitely Prince's playground. The show was so fast moving it was almost too much to keep up with - There were small sections of medleys of songs that seemed like mini concerts in themselves, paired with multiple costume changes. A bed appeared and disappeared during 'superfunkicalifragisexy' snippets of 'Controversy', 'Delirious' and 'Sister' with an awesome guitar solo. Prince played all the roles - bandleader, axe god, flirt, dancer extraordinaire and then crown joker with a hilarious take on 'Bob George' where he donned oversized sunglasses clowning around the stage with fake gunshots and police chase. As if this wasn't enough drama, the first half of the set ended with the sublime 'Anna Stesia' - the gorgeous, sweeping, emotional piano lead momentum building song right in the middle of the 'Lovesexy' album. I had felt that the first half could have closed after 'Bob George' but just as I was contending with that brilliance, Prince took it up another level - if that was at all possible. 'Anna Stesia' was presented with Prince playing solo - spotlight firmly focused on him as he strikes the first piano chord 'have you ever been so lonely that you think that you were the only one in the world' - Prince cut a lonely figure on the stage - surrounded by thousands of worshipping fans. Here he was giving a sermon - The focus was on his actions, his movements, his words. 'Love is god, god is love, girls and boys, you gotta love god above'. As if engulfed by a higher presence, he began to rise and rise - closer to God. And then silence. The first half was over - It had lasted just over an hour - it seemed a lifetime but passed in the blink of an eye. I tried to rationalise what I had witnessed and put some kind of order to it - Not easy. The multi-layered stage act was pure theatre itself- the choreography and timing exquisite. Hearing the songs live in new arrangements gave a different reverence to listening on vinyl and this was Prince - He was there. I was there. We were in the same room together - not a photo, or a video, or a TV broadcast - This was him!

Amongst all this, it's worth noting that George Clinton was introduced for a guest slot halfway through the first set - I wasn't quite sure who he was with his crazy hair, but I would find out through the course of time his excellence and relevance. At two points during the show, there were objects cascading down from the arena ceiling - fake money and imitation carnations - I managed to keep one of each, and still have to this day - unique and very memorable souvenirs. So much so, that I was asked to talk about these treasures and my Prince collection in general, as part of an online collaboration produced by the local BBC studio and overseen by my friend Steve Drayton in January 2016 - Just four months before Prince's death.

During the interval between sets, I struck up a few conversations with fellow fans around me, such was my frenzied haze of emotional crescendo. Someone mentioned how the second half was better than the first. This wasn't comprehensible was it? As the lights dimmed again, the familiar orchestrations of Clare Fisher played out over the P.A. whilst softly spoken words somewhat angelically recited the term 'cross the line 'followed almost instantaneously by 'Welcome to the New Power Generation, the reason my voice is so clear is there's no smack in my head' and we're off again! The second half was a harder, more energetic performance, if that was feasible - A tour through the 'Lovesexy' albums up tempo' high points, including a frenetic dancing performance from Cat and Prince. 'Lovesexy' itself sounded even more joyous and uplifting and spirited than it did on vinyl. The mood and pace changed slightly with 'The Cross' which rocked into a frenzy of guitar and emotion - It possibly filled the whole of London with its vast soaring crescendo. Looking at some of the set lists from the UK shows, it appears that good fortune rained down on those present on August 3rd, 1988. Not only did Prince duet with George Clinton, but he performed a solo piano set just before the main 'hits' encore. Prince would do this sporadically, and it's difficult to tease out any reason behind why he would do this for some shows, but not all. Perhaps this shouldn't be dwelt upon, and just indulged for what it was - a genius at work. Prince played snippets of songs in there most rudimentary form - 'The Ladder', 'Condition of The Heart', 'Strange Relationship' - You could almost sense how the songs may have been conceived. Prince seemed in perfect bliss with the crowd eating out of the palm of his hand - captivated.

He wasn't finished - the big hitters came out, and finally 'Alphabet Street' - Our journey was complete - The trip of a lifetime. And off they went, Cat, Sheila and Prince, circling the stage on the T - bird - waving and swaying in a very upbeat mode 'we love y'all' Prince told us. And, it was over. An intoxicating experience which, once it had settled, made me crave for more, I could not have comprehended how explosive a performance this could have been and, I was moved to tears. It felt like a lifetime's ambition had been achieved by the ripe old age of 16. When we eventually got back to Newcastle at five in the morning, Darran and I had no option but to walk home from the town centre - There were no buses at such an early hour and neither of us could afford a taxi. This was no problem, as it gave us the opportunity (although, by this point slightly fatigued) to relive the experience over and over. I got back home at 6am - somewhat disorientated. I put on the bootleg cassette of the Lovesexy show and wept again - The concert was an experience almost beyond me. My dad came into the room around 7am, I'm guessing slightly relieved that I had made it back unscathed. We talked about my feelings and how blown away I had been. In a rare melancholic moment, my dad mentioned how he was never able to see his idols, Buddy Holly and Elvis Presley. I felt for him - the experience was something, in my opinion, everyone should have been exposed to at one point in their lives - euphoric joy. Of course, it's perfectly plausible that my dad got this from another source, unfortunately just not from seeing his musical Idols.

The magic of television provided a perfect reminder of the Lovesexy tour when a delayed broadcast of one of the shows from Germany was shown on two occasions later in 1988, in edited form. As the content was slightly adult themed, the Sunday lunchtime repeat presented a few different and 'safer' songs, and with the advantage of dual video recorders I was able to edit the two together to get as much of the concert as possible. I even made my own video box for the tape and was quite pleased with my efforts. Clearly Prince's marketing team didn't fancy my utilisation of graphics, as when the show was officially released on home video, the cover art of the Lovesexy album was replicated as cover art.

As a footnote to the 1988 extravaganza, the Sign O the Times film was released across the UK late August (it had spent a month running at the dominion theatre on London's Tottenham Court Road in July). Darran and I got in to see the press screening in Newcastle which took place one Tuesday morning. We didn't quite see it all, but enough to conclude that this was another example of Prince exerting himself in the live forum. It was great to see what we missed out on the previous year, safe in the knowledge that the Lovesexy shows were in fact better.

And there was our first summer of Prince, which technically should be classed as the second, following 1984's conquest. But 1988 was the year Prince ruled - dig?

Prince would tour the UK many more times in his life, and most occasions I was fortunate to get tickets to go to shows. In total I saw Prince eight times in concert and at two after shows, which took me to double figures. I feel this is quite an achievement - I appreciate that many more people will have been more dedicated and financially blessed which enabled multiple attendances of his UK tours (and in some cases global shows), but the ten I achieved will live with me forever. Each performance was different, each tour included new songs, and the back catalogue pillared of tracks that would assist with the flow of the set list. Of course, there were the 'standards' that the casual concert goer wanted to hear, and more often than not, he obliged.

The 1990 'Nude' tour was very much a 'greatest hits' package, which incorporated tracks from the highly successful 'Batman' album released in 1989. This was presented as a 'stripped back' (hence 'Nude') show, a lot less reliant on the theatrical presentations of the previous two tours (not least of all due to the fact the schedules in 87, and more so, 88/89 were financial loss makers). But hey, it's still Prince!

An incredible run of 'Nude' shows in the UK was prepared, as if Prince were again looking to repay past misdemeanours for concert cancellations. Wembley Arena would, once more, be the main venue, but this time there was also a show in the North - at Maine Road, Manchester City's football ground. The Controversy fan network was allocated 'fan tickets' for many of the shows at Wembley. My recollection is that, between us, Darran and I applied (together this time) for at least three different dates, with one of those being one I would attend on my own. How I thought this would play out practically wasn't really something I had a logical conclusion for. As it turned out, it was of little relevance as we were sent tickets for one show, and with the stage being set in a more traditional position at the end of the arena, I feared we would see very little, as we were to be seated towards the back. Extremely fortunately, the fan service was also offering 'ticket trades' for anyone who didn't get the tickets they hoped for, and this came up trumps for us. An extremely kind lady (I seem to recall she was called Terry) swapped with us and gave up her third row seats, as she was attending multiple shows. I had met Terry and her daughter at a Prince themed house party, arranged through the North East wing of the fanzine group, which had a strong North East presence. I attended this party 'in outfit' which consisted of high waisted blue trousers, white shirt with black polka dot design and my hair held back with a large faux ribbon tie. All made by the skilful and talented hands of my mother.

To say Darran and I fell on our feet with the Nude tour tickets was an understatement, and it was all thanks to an incredible act of kindness. Our luck was most certainly in when Wendy and Lisa announced they would play two shows at the Town and Country Club in Kentish Town (also in London), the second being the night after we were to see Prince at Wembley. Once again, with huge support from our parents (although Darran was working at this point), we were able to fund, what seemed like the trip of a lifetime - Prince, Wendy and Lisa, London - Purple music frenzy!!!

On this visit to London, we would have to stay over, in a hotel, which would represent the first time since cub camp at primary school that I was to be away from home, overnight, without my parents or grandparents. I generally didn't like being away overnight, but felt this was the right thing to do, at the right time, for a tangible reward - to see Prince. Travel would be by coach, although this time by National Express, and not a private hire. It was a long, drawn out journey, yet amazingly we found our way around the metropolis of central London and got from our coach station to the hotel, which was just off Piccadilly Circus. Getting to Wembley would be a bit of a challenge as it was quite a journey on the underground. To pass some of the time pre-gig, Darran suggested we go for a drink. Darran was very much into the club scene in Newcastle, as it was in the late 80's/early 90's. Alcohol wasn't something I had really taken to at this stage of my life, save for some home brew and the odd glass of cider. I recall one potential explanation being that during a period of adolescent insomnia, it was suggested to my mother that I take a drink at some point before retiring to bed for the night. My mother took this advice and purchased a can of Kestrel lager, which I understand was very low strength. I took one sip and thought it was the most disgusting vile taste imaginable and couldn't drink anymore. I presume most people think this the first time they taste alcohol. I had brief and minimal flirtations with booze up to that point and wasn't enamoured with either the taste or the effects. Darran felt otherwise and seeing as we were 'on holiday' I concurred, and off we went to a 'proper' London boozer, in the afternoon!

My memory is that the bar staff wouldn't serve me - hardly surprising as I cut a quite unmasculine figure, short of stature, shoulder length hair and incredibly thin - in fact, there were occasions when I had been mistaken for a female. I probably didn't help my cause by asking for something along the lines of 'a small cup of beer, please' Therefore it was up to Darran to bail us out. I think I had two pints, but they may have been halves. We got another when we were inside the arena - after all, the tube journey had proved thirsty work! I didn't feel too affected, but I clearly was, as I would discover later in the evening. Once inside the arena, we were stunned to find how close we were to the stage, and therefore, how near Prince would be to us. Pre-show entertainment was offered in the form of the full-length video of Prince's upcoming single 'Thieves in the Temple' being played on large video screens, which were hung from the arena ceiling. The video looked incredible, and the full-length version would be something I would struggle to see again for several years.

As the show came nearer to opening, a montage of clips from Prince tracks played out as an intro, including the end section of 'Partyup' from the Dirty Mind album 'you're gonna have to fight your own damn war, coz we don't wanna fight no more' merged into excerpts from 'Housequake' and spoken sections from the 'Batman' soundtrack, which then flew into the opening number 'The Future' - a dark drum pattern complimented by a Clare Fischer arrangement was the backdrop intro to the Prince movie on show tonight.. And there he was dressed in black and white in front of the huge lettering which spelled 'Prince' and ready to use the fireman's pole/climbing frame on set. Darran and I were so close to him, that we were within touching distance of the plectrums he was dishing out to lucky crowd goers. As ever, he was full of quips/banter and smiles - lots of smiles - he always appeared incredibly happy on stage, no matter what the size of the arena. The set list itself may not have contained as many surprises as the 'Lovesexy' shows and, in all honesty, I could never really get away with the 'Game Boyz' used as backing singers/dancers. But Prince still excelled as a live artist, and presenting 'greatest hits' seemed de rigueur in 1990, as David Bowie was also touring large venues with his 'Sound and Vision' shows, very much drawing on pat incarnations and fan favourites, as opposed to the more conceptual showcases of the recent past.

Once again, elated post show, we made our way back to the tube for the return journey to central London. This is where events took a downturn. The tube station was not sparse, and it seemed like most of the crowd attending the show were using this mode of transport, at the same time. It had been a hot day, we had travelled from Newcastle. I had had little to eat but had consumed three alcoholic beverages. I was feeling increasingly nauseous and, on a cramped train back, could see no other option. I was going to be sick in my rolled-up Prince poster. I think I got as far as placing the poster towards my mouth and just hoped for the best, when the train pulled into a station suddenly and with an exodus of passengers and a huge draft of cool air, I suddenly felt better. I don't know what was more satisfying - my symptom resolution, or the fact that the poster remained intact. It was, after all, a life size door hanging one of Prince, which I still have (fully intact) to this day!

Following our London adventure, Darran and I hastily booked up a coach and concert package to go to the Maine Road show. Seeing Prince was very much a drug, and we wanted as many hits as we could get. By the time this show came around, Prince would have a new album in the shops - 'Graffiti Bridge' which supported a film release - the much anticipated follow up to 'Purple Rain' reuniting the characters 'The Kid' and Morris. The Time were reforming, although the Revolution were not. Prince had included new track 'The Question of U' from the album and film in his current tour set. A deep blues-based ballad with a signature Prince guitar solo, this boded well for the album, which would be a double, and, unlike 'Purple Rain' would include all the acts that were featured in the film on the soundtrack release.

Whilst this helped me look forward to the show in Manchester, there was to be an unexpected turn that would see me think twice about going. A few weeks before our trip to Manchester, Darran announced that he was moving to Edinburgh, to secure a job and wouldn't now be able to get to Manchester. This was a bit of surprise and left me a little stunned. I would retain contact with Darran, and remain very close to him, but this was an end of innocence moment - all the times we had shared listening to music, going to town to buy records, watching music videos was over. Of course, this was natural - people grow up, and, at a couple of years older than me, it was inevitable that we would move in different social circles at some point. I don't remember a big send off, but I remember (perhaps a bit selfishly) thinking what I would do about the Manchester show. I had been to one or two small gigs on my own by now - I had left school and was attending college, and, very much finding 'alternative' music a big draw. I had my own bass guitar and was looking to form a band myself. However, travelling to a concert as large as the Maine Road event, on my own was perhaps a step too far but then, this was Prince. I don't recall talking it over, but I did take some inspiration from an experience my dad had told me about. Apparently, in the 60's he had won a competition. The prize was a ticket to see the Beatles at Newcastle City Hall. There was only one ticket, and as he didn't want to go on his own, my dad turned down the prize. Now I have never been a fan of the Beatles, but a free ticket to see them in my hometown? At least if I'd gone and not liked it, it would have been a story to tell. My dad had his reasons, and I respect that, but I was pretty determined not to let going to an event on my own stop me from going. Well, not at this point in my life. It's true my view has changed a bit on this. There are times when I've ducked out of events simply because I've no-one to go with and there have been one or two regrets. Prince in Manchester wasn't going to be one in 1990!

There was to be a familiar feeling at this concert - It was a hot late summer's day and my ticket was a general admission one, which meant standing on the pitch. This seemed ok, as I sat pre-gig, on the covered grass and ate some of the sandwiches my mam had made and packed for me. Less so, when the support band (Lois Lane) came on and everyone stood up and didn't sit back down again. I, once more, began to feel nauseous and slightly faint, not helped by the mass of long hair I had at the time. Cups of water were passed around and I utilised the cartons of juice in my 'survival pack' from my mam. As the sun began to set, so the temperature dropped, and it was quite cool when Prince came on stage, and, quite hot from a show point of view. My view was obviously obscured at many points during the performance, but the way the stage was lit up against the night sky was picturesque and vibrant. The sound too, carried well. It may not have been the most personal of shows, but I still lapped it up, as well as some 'unofficial' merchandise outside of the stadium. Getting back to Newcastle around 2am, I don't recall getting picked up and my memory tells me, once again that I walked home, feeling somewhat pleased with myself.

As a matter of fact, this was a great week for me. On the previous Saturday I had gone, with my dad to see Newcastle United thrash Leeds 5-2. That Monday saw the release of 'Graffiti Bridge' and Duran Duran's latest album 'Liberty' - whilst neither of these were the pinnacle of either artist's recording output, they each had gems contained within. The Tuesday was the Maine Road Show, and, on the Thursday, I received my best ever exam results, following a second year of taking additional subjects at college. This included an 'A' in English literature. On the Friday my Dad and I took a day trip to Jedburgh, with 'Graffiti

Bridge' and 'Liberty' on the car stereo. The week was rounded off with a small club gig by one of my favourite 'indie' bands of the time 'Jesus Jones'. Despite Darran moving, it felt, for this week, as if everything I touched turned to gold. I felt positive and having seen Prince for the third time, quite inspired. My inspiration got as far as signing on for unemployment benefit late that summer which was quite an increase in income but would ultimately lead to a further episode of depression, which saw me retreat and become quite insular, falling into a routine of staying in my bedroom for long periods, listening to music and watching videos (now having this facility to call upon myself). One of these videos was 'Graffiti Bridge' - the film which had performed so badly in the US, that it didn't warrant a cinema distribution in the UK. In all honesty, I could see why. At best, it could be viewed as 'misguided', although it does contain some great Prince performances. I don't wish to dwell on it, other than to say, even a genius can have an off day.

My memory is very often kind to me and I have no problem in recalling and remembering set lists - especially Prince ones. With one exception. I have very little recollection of the gig at Meadowbank Stadium in Edinburgh during 1993. I have good storage on getting there and back. This was to be another show I would travel to on my own, or at least that was how it was planned. Darran was to attend the show, as he lived within the vicinity, but we had arranged to meet nearby as I would pass on some Newcastle United memorabilia, given that Newcastle had just completed a successful promotion season.

As with the Sign O the Times tour, there was a polite request to wear something in a particular colour - this time purple. I was happy to oblige with a canvas purple shirt, and I also wore the symbol necklace I had purchased from the nude shows in 1990.

Setting off on the morning of the show, I secured a seat on the coach on my own and was soon joined by a fellow concert goer who also appeared to be a lone traveller. Knowing it was a fair journey ahead, I made polite conversation, but my new travelling companion soon moved on as she had located some of her friends. At least that's what she told me. I was quite surprised when she came back and asked if I wanted to sit with her group, as I was on my own! This made the journey much more tolerable and I was extremely grateful for this act of kindness. Unfortunately, I wasn't to meet with Darran before the gig as our coach was stuck in traffic following a road accident, and we arrived with not a lot of time to spare until the gates of the stadium opened. I didn't think there would be an issue with me vacating my seat and getting to the standing area where Darran had said he would be. Not so! This was not permissible, and I was turned back to my seat to observe from afar.

Prince had released two albums since 'Graffiti Bridge' and toured them. The first, 1991's 'Diamonds and Pearls' I wasn't so taken with overall - The singles released in the UK were mostly all pretty special (there were five of them - 'Gett Off', 'Cream', 'Money Don't Matter Tonight' and 'Thunder' were all gems - 'Diamonds and Pearls', less so). The overall sound of the album was less focused on drum machines and synthesisers, which Prince was synonymous with in the 80's, and had I felt, a much more noticeable rap/hip hop influence, with the high prominence of the 'Game Boyz' with this album. Prince was trying to fit in with current sounds, instead of getting current sounds to fit with his ideas. Perhaps after the commercial failure of the Graffiti Bridge project, Prince felt he needed to regain some commercial credibility. It worked with the album being his best performer in the US since 'Purple Rain'. He brought the tour to the UK, but I couldn't muster enough funds or, if I'm honest, enthusiasm to travel for an album I was generally ambivalent towards, despite it being a Prince album.

My feeling changed a lot with the 'Symbol' album which was released towards the end of 1992. Another double, this was a described as a Prince opus, and did follow a loose narrative thread. Overall, this was a much more ambitious project with Prince returning to what he did best - being Prince. Not quite up there with 'Sign O the Times', the Love symbol album did deliver a variety of styles and experiments, with techno ('I Wanna Melt With U'), reggae ('Blue Light') and a rock opera track in the vein of Queen's 'Bohemian Rhapsody'. So, with '3 Chains O Gold', 4 strong singles were released, including the criminally overlooked 'Morning Papers', although this would be the first time since 'Purple Rain' that a Prince album contained two Top Ten singles in the UK. Building on this momentum, the album also topped the charts and it seemed Prince's popularity and pulling power (in the UK at least) was still high.

For the promo to the opening track and second single from the album 'My Name is Prince' - the author and focus of the song, whilst delivering a bombastic (and, in my view, quite tongue in cheek) proclamation of his inception, he wore a hat with a sort of chain mail visa that completely covered his face. How practical that was, I'm unsure, but I do feel if I had worn a similar design at my workplace, the health and safety do gooders would have had a field day! The song actually proved ironically prophetic as Prince, in the near future was to undergo an image overhaul which would see him 'kill off' the Prince character within him.

I mentioned that my memories were not as vivid of this show, but what I can remember was the start - Prince arrived on stage wearing the aforementioned chainmail hat and proceeded to deliver a note perfect rendition of 'My Name is Prince' while being delivered to us from a swing, lowered from the sky, or so we thought. It became apparent, when the hat was removed that it was actually his dancer (and soon to be wife) Mayte, who was behind the veil...the twister! I should have suspected so as the character in the hat slipped on stage, which Prince would never do!!! Prince entered the stage somewhat casually, holding his microphone as a curtain was pulled back to reveal a backdrop of the 'Symbol' album's cover, which unfortunately also fell to the ground, revealing a new concert scene setter - the surrounding area of the stadium!

What I can remember during the show is that Prince performed 'Sign O the Times' which I had never heard him play before - I had seen live clips of the song but wasn't present when it was interjected into a set list. It seemed too odd to have an ultimate show opener inserted into the middle of a show and it was a very clipped interpretation, which Prince was prone to do with a lot of his tracks. Afforded the luxury of being able to source the setlist, I recognise that there were actually very few tracks from the current album Prince was promoting and even less from a hugely successful album he had released two years previously (Diamonds and Pearls), but in their places were some of the better known album tracks from the past ten years, intermixed with his larger UK hits. It's actually very close to an ideal setlist, for the time, even with the inclusion of the then unknown 'Endorphinemachine' and 'Come' as encores.

Amazingly, in a crowd of thousands, I bumped into Darran, post-show and was able to exchange a few words. The coach journey back to Newcastle was not so smooth, as the bus developed a puncture and we had to wait for a replacement. My mind clearly (and disappointingly) has focused in on all of the negative aspects of this concert experience. Ironically, given the setting of the next Prince performance I would attend, I can only think of the positive.

Not long after the Meadowbank show, I secured a new job. I had been out of work during the summer as the company I worked for was forced to make redundancies. I wasn't too bothered as I heavily disliked working there. This had been my first taste of 'proper' paid work, following a few years of 'signing on' (claiming benefit) and a work placement. I was still living at home with my parents and, as a matter of fact, the drop in money from my then salary to receiving benefit was not so huge.

As fate would have it, my first day in this new job would be the same date of the release of the first Prince 'greatest hits' compilation - September 13th, 1993. It was actually three compilations as there was 'Hits 1', 'Hits 2' and a 3 CD box set 'The hits and the B-sides' Strictly speaking they weren't all 'hits' and, indeed, not even all singles, but they still represented a good reflection on Prince's career to date, along with a sprinkling of new tracks ('Power Fantastic' being the clear cream of this crop). I had to have this album, on the day of release, but now being employed, and not located in the town centre, or near a record store, I couldn't guarantee I would have finished my first day in my new job before the shops closed. I needn't have worried as, rather like the first day at school, everyone got an early finish. As I was not to know in advance, I had arranged for my sister to pick up a copy of the 3-CD box set for me, which made the journey back from 'the office' much more tolerable.

In terms of the release, many of the edits of the tracks had not previously been released on CD, but the real draw of the project was the B-sides disc. Compact disc was very much the currency of music consumption now. However, the rarer tracks of Prince's career weren't available in this format, until now, so it was a joy to listen to the likes of 'Gotta Stop', 'How Come U Don't Call Me Anymore', '17 Days' and 'Hello' in this crisp, scratch free, clear audio. Not to be overlooked, is the excellent essay by Alan Leeds contained within the accompanying booklet.

Prince's consistently high creative output may have waned a little. In my view - he had seemed to lose a little bit of the edge he had during his untouchable majestic period, but his popularity showed no signs of dropping - The hits compilations sold well, and both double albums (only Prince could release two double albums, as well as a triple CD set on the same day) got into the Top 10 UK album charts on release. Oddly, I thought, 'Controversy' was re-released as a second single to promote the 'hits' campaign ('Peach' being the first). Even stranger was that it was released with no reference to the original cover art, but, this seemed to matter not a jot, as the single (promoted by the original video, just to confuse matters further), went Top 10 in the UK charts, giving Prince a sizeable hit with a song that was first released over ten years previously, and had troubled only the bargain bins of record stores.

The two part CD single was the primary format of release for singles at this point - A cunning twist on multi-formatting which was culled after saturation in the late eighties/early nineties, when chart compilers had issued strict rules that only a limited number of formats would qualify for sales inclusion, and ultimately chart position. With CD's being in the ascendency, most releases came in this medium - The thought was to release one version with a 'double sleeve' first, leaving a space for 'CD 2' which was tantalisingly not available until the following week, thus boosting second week sales as a number of fans, very much including me, would not like to see an empty portion of a CD box! Just to complete the scene, 'Controversy' was also released on 7-inch picture disc, carrying a picture from the 'Hits' photo session.

All of this was playing out in my new workplace surroundings which was a shift in what I had experienced during my brief working career to date. Yes, it was 'office work' but the office was not secluded and contained many more people that I had worked with in the past, together. There was a high value on socialising, which, completely against my character, in the main, I was happy to do. This seemed a good opportunity to meet new people - work, by and large, was secondary. This was a fun place to work, even if the work itself was not fun at all. Football was very high on the agenda for discussion, with Newcastle United being one of the most (if not the most) exciting teams to watch at the time. This fitted the era like a glove. I had attended football matches with my dad since I was 9-years-old and followed football and sport in general throughout my life. In fact, it would be safe to say that at this period, following football (and Newcastle United) defined me. But music was always there - and Prince was always there, despite the two not really complimenting each other (Prince was very much seen as a 'puff' by the majority of the masculine football crowd, in fact, on one occasion when I chose to put 'Kiss' on the video jukebox in a pub, post football, I heard him described as a 'darkie puff'). Besides not many Prince songs lend themselves to being sung as popular terrace chants.

There was to be salvation afoot - I was to meet someone who would become a very close friend and was as fanatical about elements of Prince's career. Mark was a bona fide Prince follower - like Darran, he was older, but this time, 8 years was the difference - in fact, Mark celebrated his 30th birthday in the very week I began working with him (an occasion marked by a two hour lunch break in a local public house that Friday, which would become a staple fixture in the working week, often to be followed with a continuation of drinking, after an early finish on a Friday). Mark was quite a quiet character, so, despite my laddish outgoing (and ultimately false) demeanour, I could empathise with him - more so when we struck up a conversation about music and Mark let slip he was a Prince fan. I was later to uncover that Mark had been a DJ, and therefore was able to tap into Prince much earlier than I had (although my age was a bit against me!).This also meant that not only did Mark like music, but he understood it the way I did - chart placings, B-sides, 'family trees' - he got it, in a way that very few people I have connected with do. Not since conversation with Darran had I been able to freely discuss the merits of some of the Prince protégé albums and Prince bootlegs/outtakes. I would learn a lot from Mark in many lessons of 'musicology', not least of all the 70's UK 'glam/art' scene as Mark was a huge fan of David Bowie and Roxy Music, two acts that I had only real knowledge of from 80's chart hits. Mark was able to enunciate and contextualise the early periods for both acts and recommend albums that I should hear (I recall with great affection, the lengthy telephone conversation we had about David Bowie's back catalogue when I was keen to explore and uncover the delights of his shapeshifting personas of the 70's). In return, I was updating Mark on a lot of current bands, so there was a cross over, given that this was the Britpop era where Bowie and Roxy directly, or otherwise were cited as influences. I was stunned to learn that Mark had seen Prince at Wembley arena in 1986 (as well as 1988), although he did confess to not thinking much of the Batman project. Years later, he remarked with what I took as a backhanded compliment by saying that he thought he had the North East Prince market cornered, until he met me! Very soon into our friendship, Mark, I, and assorted others attended football matches and gigs together. The differentiation and separation between work and play was extremely blurred and it was difficult, at times to see where one stopped and the other started. Inevitably (at least to me) Mark and I would see Prince together, although it was probably not his highest profile tour.

Following on from the 'Hits' collection, Prince's next project was the single 'The Most Beautiful Girl In The World' released on his own NPG label. This release was significant in many ways, not least of which was the fact it gave Prince his only UK Number 1 single. However, Prince was firmly in a battle with his label Warner Brothers, who, it seemed would not let Prince have complete artistic control over his output. Prince had a new album 'The Gold Experience' recorded and ready to be unleashed, but his record company wanted a bit more 'life' out of previous albums and would prefer Prince to space out his albums a bit more, with numerous singles taken from each album. Prince did not want to work this way, and, as is often journaled, was frequently two albums down the line in terms of writing and recording whilst the project he had finished six months ago was only just being released. This dispute became very bitter with Prince proclaiming his displeasure at his employer very publicly, appearing with the word 'Slave' written across his face. The rights and wrongs of this have been debated elsewhere. What struck me, as a fan was that Prince appeared to be alienating himself from the common man, although I did admire him for speaking his mind. I was also upset that a lot of Prince recordings were being held back in the name of profiteering. I was a fan, if Prince wanted me to hear his new albums, did I not have the right to do so? Prince ultimately would answer this with a 'yes' - as long as you subscribe to my internet only release schedule. I didn't.

In early 1995 it was announced that Prince would tour the UK... except he wouldn't - having distanced himself from the identity that was 'Prince', he was now to be referred to as the symbol he had adopted as his moniker...despite the fact it could not be pronounced. Therefore, he became known as 'The artist formerly known as Prince' or any derivative, complimentary, or otherwise. Once again, there was to be a show in Manchester, and the availability of a coach and concert package from Newcastle City Hall. I don't think I had to sell this much to Mark, as he was always eager to travel to football matches or concerts. I might have struggled if I had openly informed Mark of Prince's notification to fans that he wouldn't be playing any of his 'hits' - but I thought, this is Prince - he NEVER disappoints live. In all honesty, he didn't. Not in my eyes, at least - Yes, the set was made up predominantly of songs I hadn't heard until that point, but there was a section where he did play some well-known tracks (although not classic hits, admittedly), and to hear him sing 'I Love U In Me' (a B-side) was simply worth going for alone. I didn't think there was a great atmosphere at the show, but, then again, I'm sure a lot of people were still hopeful he would do '1999' and 'Purple Rain'. Arguably the show could have been classed as self-indulgent, but I chose not to see that - I was simply excited to get my hands on these songs, as well as the promo films that were shown at the beginning of the night on big screens. Prince may not have been playing his hits tonight, but I still felt he was on fire and pulled off a great performance, which included an outing of his 'symbol' guitar. I was in somewhat of a minority as a slightly subdued coach found its way back to Newcastle from Manchester. I didn't care for some of the comments I heard, and some of them actually took a personal angle as I had attended the show with a semi Prince outfit, wearing eyeliner. It was a tough time to be a Prince fan, and, in all honesty, Prince didn't help himself with appearances on UK TV to talk about the shows where he would be 'interviewed' with a scarf over his face, refusing to answer any questions and choosing only to whisper responses in Mayte's ear who would then translate to the camera. Worse was to come - Warner's released a cringe worthy 'megamix' to gain some revenue from the tour where Prince had no new album to promote. This was far from ideal. Prince and Warner's agreed to an amicable(ish) separation, and Prince was ultimately free to release what he wanted, when he wanted. As part of this severance package, the 'Black' album finally got an official, limited release, along with 'The Gold Experience' in the autumn of 1995. I found this to be an exceptional album, and one which saw Prince back on form - many of the songs from the Manchester show were here in cleaner, more polished versions, contained within an extremely coherent set.

Prince continued his release schedule with an album which on first listen I was quite dismissive of, but coming back to it years later, I actually found to be a hidden gem - the guitar heavy 'Chaos and Disorder' this was followed not quite six months later by a triple CD selection 'Emancipation' - At this point I couldn't keep up, and finding the time alone to listen to three hours of new Prince music was a challenge - the days of sitting in my bedroom day after day/night after night were long gone - I was working full time and quite often at weekends too. Any other time was generally given to socialising. However, persevere I did, and, in all honesty, 'Emancipation' is not a bad album - it is simply over ambitious and would have served better as, at most, a double CD.

There were very few Prince Shows throughout the UK during this period. Indeed, it would be some 12 years between me attending Prince Concerts. Not that Prince didn't visit, more so that I wasn't particularly aware of it, with one notable exception.

Prince never played a full on gig in Newcastle, although there were some rumours that venues in the region had been looked into for the 2014 Hit n Run shows. This did not materialise. So, the only visit that I am aware of was to play a one off 'Tube' special toward the end of 1999.

The Tube was a groundbreaking music show, broadcast from Tyne Tees studios, in Newcastle which ran during the early to mid-eighties. It was anarchic and, as it was broadcast live, somewhat unpredictable. It ended in 1987 with Duran Duran being the last band to play. However, there was to be a special, to celebrate the end of the millennium, and Prince was to be the star attraction. This I couldn't quite believe - Prince in Newcastle? Where on earth would he stay? Would he be prepared for the harsh weather? (I'm guessing coming from Minneapolis he had experienced one or two cold spells). The big question I asked myself, however, was how would I get to see him? Tickets were likely to be hard to come by, if available at all.

It seemed somewhat ironic that Prince was coming to Newcastle in 1999 - the title of one of his most recognisable and noteworthy breakthrough singles. He'd actually re-recorded the track and put it out as 'the new master' to perhaps counter Warner's decision to re-release the original track at the turn of the year, which actually gave him his last UK Top 10 hit in his lifetime.

1999 had been a challenging and eventful one for me - the year Prince wrote as bringing the end of the world, certainly felt it, personally. The year started off very well, as I would move into Mark's property and rent a couple of room's off him - this saw a great deal of happy, fun and hedonistic times for us both, given we were both single, living away from home and in full time employment (Mark was actually working two jobs). The house Mark owned was in a very affluent area of Newcastle. In the bedroom I stayed in I decorated the wall with some framed prints - one of which had to be of Prince. For around six months, the house was full of laughter and alcohol (not always mutually exclusive), which probably peaked with an early summer barbeque in May 1999 to 'celebrate' Newcastle United getting to the F.A. Cup final, which inevitably, they lost. I had been there, at Wembley to witness the capitulation of the team, in front of a national audience of television viewers on the occasion of the 'showpiece' of the English domestic football season. There was also a new 'Star Wars' film out this year

- a prequel. We all attended as a family, just as we had in 1977 in the same theatre (my dad, mam, and sister Margaret joined by her then fiancé Andy) - My dad sat next to me in the packed cinema, asking if I wanted him to read out the text at the beginning of the story, as he had when I was five at the original film.

In July of that year, my dad took unwell, He needed to go to hospital to have some tests and asked me to drive him as I was off work. I couldn't as I had been drinking early in the afternoon, whilst on a day's leave. Later that week my dad was admitted to hospital to have some further tests run. It was July 30th. He was admitted to the hospital where, coincidentally I was working in a p*ss boring admin job, which was made a lot more tolerable due to the camaraderie between members of the team. This would have advantages and disadvantages.

My dad died in the Freeman Hospital on the 21st, August 1999. Three weeks after his admission. He returned home briefly, on weekend leave, but ultimately would pass away in a side room on the ward. There are many events that have changed the course of my life and sent me reeling into long battles with depression. This was one. My dad is never far from my thoughts and I miss him every day of my life. Just as I miss knowing Prince is alive. Losing my dad is something I have never recovered from, I simply live with it and have adapted to life without him, as difficult as it is. The two deaths are connected, but different. Both were men I admired and looked to and took inspiration from. Both guided me and helped shape me (directly or indirectly) into the person I am today. Without either in my life, I would not be writing these thoughts, as trite as they perhaps read.

That Prince would be in Newcastle months after my own father's death was not lost - It felt as if he was coming to see me, to tell me, again 'things will be alright' to not stop believing, to remain focussed and positive. He didn't tell me these things, of course and I didn't get to the show, although I did catch a glimpse of him walking around the studio - the back of him, but it was unmistakably Prince - no one else could be that small and carry off the high heels and shoulder length hair look, yet still appear heterosexually masculine. Surrounded by security and from a distance (I had taken the decision to go down to the television studio building and loiter outside in the hope of seeing him), it could quite easily not have been him, but I don't dwell on that outcome too much - In my eyes, I had seen him, and, as fleeting a sighting as it was, it would do, for now.

The longest period between me seeing Prince in concert, it would be fair to say, was a time of mixed fortunes for him. From 1995 to 2007 album releases that were freely available by traditional methods became fewer and fewer, although his output increased, more in keeping with his vision of delivering music to his fans. Prince was one of the first artists to offer an Internet based subscription only service where fans were given the opportunity to access a number of releases. I didn't subscribe - I had no internet access. By this time, I was living on my own and without a computer, the Internet was a bit of a pipe dream, for now. Prince's personal life also saw fluctuations. He married Mayte on February 14th, 1996 (my 24th birthday, which, of course, made it feel like some sort of distant connection). Sadly, the couple's one and only child died days after his birth, with mystery and rumour surrounding the unfortunate and tragic circumstances of the infant's passing.

Prince opened a retail store in Camden, London, which I regrettably did not visit. My vision of this would be that it sold all of Prince's records and concert films, including all of the unreleased ones in pristine condition. I don't think that was the reality with the store appearing to be a high end clothing boutique. Still, should have made more effort to visit, if, for nothing more than a carrier bag.

The albums Prince chose (or his record company chose) to issue for public consumption were, patchy. 'Rave Un2 the Joy Fantastic' reprised a song originally based around the 'Batman' project and that album contained a couple of gems 'Baby Knows' and 'The Greatest Romance Ever Sold' – There was little else of note, other than the fact he was now recording and releasing as 'Prince' again, albeit with a different label (arista). Indeed, Prince became very much a roaming recording artist, signing, it seemed, short-term, one album distribution deals. 'The Rainbow Children' was very much an experimental jazz/fusion album, although this time more conceptual that he had been since the 'Love Symbol' album. It took me a long time to love this album, partly due to the slightly off putting narrative voice throughout the album, which was Prince manipulated and slowed down this time (as per 'Scarlett Pussy' from the 'I Wish U Heaven' single). Prince also released an instrumental album 'N.E.W.S.' further down the line, which I did get, and loved as it had more of an extended Madhouse feel to it. He also wrote music that was used at his wedding to Mayte ('Karma Sutra' which was labelled as a ballet) and a proposed musical 'Glam Slam Ulysses' which name checked the nightclub he opened in venues across the United States.

Prince toured the 'Rainbow Children' album under the 'One Night Alone' (actually the title of an internet only piano album) moniker - This tour visited the UK and saw Prince play much smaller, intimate venues. Such was the lack of credible Prince news in the music papers at the time, that, without the Internet, I was not aware that this happened until many years after. I would have to wait until 2007 until I next had the chance to attend a Prince concert, and even then, it almost didn't happen.

In 2004, Prince released the album (and single) Musicology via RCA - a major label. This gave Prince a huge hit album in the US - helped in no small way by the issuing of free copies of the CD at his concerts across the county. More coherent than for some time, the album had some great tracks - The title track, a true funk workout in paying homage to Prince's musical influences sounded fresh, yet classic Prince. 'Dear Mr Man' was a wonderful reflective tune about the state of the world and 'Call My Name' a standard ballad, but done very, very well. On the intro to 'Illusion, Coma, Pimp and Circumstance' (my favourite on the album) there were excerpts of some of Prince's hits in a sort of radio tuning effect (Prince would actually return to the theme of revisiting some of his previous tracks, later in his career). The album received the most positive reviews Prince had received for some time, and he seemed now comfortable playing the 'crowd pleasers' of the past in fuller format, to larger, stadium sized crowds. This was good PR for Prince, and he was now being recognised as a 'heritage' artist. He seemed to have found a happy medium, acknowledging the desire for older and casual fans to hear the 'hits' at large shows, but also using the funding and exposure this provided to enable him to push still relevant and creative pieces. In 2006 he was honoured at the Brits Awards for 'outstanding achievement' (ironic, given that 21 years earlier he had been ridiculed for his appearance at the award ceremony) and he performed with Sheila E a medley of hits and new tracks. He released his second album in two years '3121' - Again on a major label. This time Columbia. This album contained the dirt hot 'Black Sweat' which drew on 'Let's Work' as a point of reference but updated the sound. To me, it sounded, once again like classic Prince and deserved widespread success. Unfortunately, this wasn't to happen - the singles market had shifted, as, indeed had record sales in general - Very few artists made profit from releases, with live shows and direct selling (often via the Internet) being the main areas of profit.

Prince's 'Brit' set was reprised during the Super Bowl halftime show in early 2007. This drew a record number of viewers and showed that Prince still had huge pulling power, albeit for songs he had, in general, released over 20 years ago. Prince knew what he was doing, and it seemed slightly ironic to me that he was now in such good stock, given the lack of support he had received for some of his albums which slipped under the radar. It seemed there was a hard core of fans who would buy anything he released (hands up from me!!) yet an equally (and possibly larger) pure nostalgia crowd who wanted to hear 'Purple Rain', '1999', etc. Prince's skill was that he managed to please pretty much both camps, and I lapped it all up. I loved seeing him on TV, he was happy to be interviewed and seemed candid, relaxed, and dare I say it 'normal'!!!

He also looked amazing - his skin appeared untarnished, he dressed stylishly and appropriately, but still with the mystique and flair of an untouchable. Despite his calmness and relatively outgoing demeanour, I was never in any doubt that Prince still operated outside of the world I know. He may have shifted his dwelling from 'Paisley Park' to '3121' (an apartment he apparently was renting, which gave the name to his current album) but, in my eyes and thoughts it didn't matter - Prince lived in 'Prince World'. He perfectly permitted access to this area via his albums and tours, but he only gave what he wanted. His air of invincibility was palpable, no more so than in the live setting. If anyone is ever in any doubt about this, look at the clip from the show during which he was inducted into the Rock 'n' Roll Hall of Fame (2004), where he shares a stage with guitar greats Jeff Lynne, Tom Petty and Steve Winwood as they pay homage to George Harrison, playing his 'While My Guitar Gently Weeps'. In the company of, perhaps, more conventional artists, and certainly more leaning toward the 'establishment' or 'safe' end of rock, Prince takes them all with an astounding virtuoso performance, which I understand was spontaneous...His colleagues on stage appear astounded.

To capitalise on this renaissance in his popularity, Prince, in early 2007, announced he would play 21 nights as part of his 'Earth Tour' at the soon to open 02 Arena in Greenwich Peninsula, London. This was quite a statement, more so when the ticket price was announced at 31.21 British pounds and pence, which would include a copy of the as yet unreleased new Prince album. I couldn't miss out on this opportunity, could I? Unfortunately, the initial answer was yes. I was in between house moves and had moved back to my mother's house, whilst the proposed new home for my fiance (Lorraine) and myself was stuck in a housing sale chain. Yes, I had money in the bank, following the sale of my flat, but this was a much lower profit margin that I had hoped. And, with solicitor's fees and more outgoings for storage of furniture etc, I was left with little that I could utilise, given that a new house was imminent, coupled with the need for a replacement car. Darran was equally unable to commit - the price of the tickets was favourable, but the travel and accommodation were the limiting factors. A reflection of our situations and increased responsibilities, we conclude that it just isn't meant to be this time.

As the dates come closer and closer, there was still limited ticket availability. Prince, it is announced, is to release the new album accompanying his shows - 'Planet Earth' via a giveaway with a national Sunday newspaper. This is unprecedented - usually these 'cover mounts' are rehashes of old releases, compilations or live versions. Never before has a brand new studio album been offered in this way. My initial thoughts are of regret - have things really got so bad for Prince that he has to give away his new album? Will it really not sell? Reflecting back, this was a very calculated and wise move. Prince would have received a one off payment from the newspaper, whose circulation would have increased - thus meaning that the album would be in the hands of people who possibly were unaware that Prince was still recording, or, indeed, who he was. This would add, at least curiosity value, and inevitably lead to an upsurge (to some degree) of back catalogue sales. The album itself was actually very good, and I have a lot of time for it (not so much when the idea was replicated for the weaker '2010' album, three years later, which equally didn't have the impact of the 'Planet Earth' marketing and saw a number of remaining copies of the album given away with local newspapers). The title track saw Prince reunite on record with Wendy and Lisa and the harmonies provided really complimented the track, although this did beg the question as to why the collaboration was limited to just one track. Further aces were served via the bouncy radio single 'Guitar', 'The One You Wanna C' and ultimately with the R&B tight funk of 'Chelsea Rodgers' - the bass line of which felt like the whole of the world was moving, such was its heaviness. With momentum gathering ahead of Prince's summer visit to the UK, I re-evaluated. I should, at least attempt to attend one of the shows - It seemed like the correct thing to do, and so what if I couldn't go on holiday that year? That, after all, was a luxury, wasn't it, and given the choice, what would I rather do? (as it happens, I did holiday that year).

Speaking to Lorraine, it was clear she also would like to attend, and we could make a sort of mini break of it. My sister too, and her partner were keen, and of course Darran would join us, I assumed. Coincidentally, at this stage of her career, my sister was working for a ticketing agency and was able to look at availability for the whole run of shows. As leave from work was precious, we would need to go on a weekend, which wasn't difficult to secure. It would be the first Saturday show. In the run up to the residency, Prince also announced that there would be an after show performance at the smaller club venue Indigo2 within the complex. Prince's appearance and performance would not be guaranteed on any of these nights, but this was certainly a carrot dangling operation that worked for me - I snapped up two tickets for the after show as well. After show performances were the stuff of legend in Prince circles - especially in the late 80's where it was pretty much the norm for Prince to do a two and a half hour set in a large arena, then skip across town to an unannounced small club venue and perform a different set, again lasting a couple of hours, well into the morning. These impromptu sets always seemed untouchable and were often attended by the beautiful people who may or may not have been tipped off that Prince was likely to play in a certain local, on a specified night. There is an idealistic romantic notion in my mind, which is lost, to a degree with Prince taking up residency at Indigo2, in that I liked the idea of him being transported across a city and picking out a venue, at will, when the desire took him over and he just felt he needed to play more music. The reality is that there must have been a level of organisation, not least of all to ensure that Prince would be playing to a packed crowd!

Lorraine was able to secure us a room for the night in what seemed, at the time, as the only hotel within walking distance of the 02. This was ideal for us, as it meant we wouldn't have to worry about leaving a Prince performance to get the last tube back across London. Six tickets were booked for the performance in the main arena on Saturday August 4th. Darran just couldn't make it, so a colleague from work would take the two tickets that were allocated to him. Lorraine and I travelled down on the Saturday morning via train. I had been living on a staple diet of Prince albums and watching back all the concert footage I had (which was, at this point, quite considerable), in preparation - even reliving 'Under the Cherry Moon' with Lorraine the night before the journey - not that she was particularly impressed! I had been in preparation for this visit, picking out an outfit, and making sure I was able to wear it well. I locked myself in our garage for a period before our evening meal every night to undergo a fitness regime, just to ensure I was going to look my best. It was as if I was performing myself! I located my 1988 Lovesexy T-shirt, which was a bit musty, but still fitted (If anything, it was too big and unshaped, given that I had purposely bought it 'extra-large' at the time, and, after years of being packed away, it hadn't aged particularly well). I also loaned a faux leather jacket from Mark to complete the outfit and would finish the look with subtle use of eyeliner.

Lorraine had been a casual fan of Prince, but was eager to see him live, and also keen to be there with me to experience the thrill of me seeing my idol. If anything, I felt more excited that I had almost 20 years ago for the Lovesexy show. A lot had happened since then, in both Prince's life and mine. He hadn't done shows this big in the country for over ten years, and he was very much in the ascendancy of popularity again. Anticipation was back in fashion, as we travelled down, arriving at the 02 complex on Saturday afternoon.

On the approach to the arena via the stairs to the underground, there were noticeably lots of images of Prince in the advertising hoardings. My desire to be at that concert seemed to be going up a notch every minute - What would he play? How would he start? The reviews of the opening night of the run had all been complementary, with Simon Price of The Independent newspaper writing a brilliant review from a fanboy perspective that I warmed to with every word. Prince had promised to mix up his sets, and not do the same order of songs or selection in any two shows. He actually began the 21 run show with 'Purple Rain'...NO WAY - talk about throwing the rule book (admittedly his own) out of the window!

Once again, the weather in London was hot and sunny. We passed the afternoon by watching 'The Simpsons' film in a nearby multiplex. I needed a drink to calm me down. Margaret was yet to arrive with Colin as they were driving from their home in Liverpool and staying a couple of stops away from the arena. After a couple of drinks, Lorraine and I left our hotel for the arena - it was a short walk in terms of distance, but it felt like it took forever to actually arrive at the venue. More images of Prince passed us en-route, and more and more people were making their way to what looked like a large circus tent. Many concert goers sat outside the venue, revelling in the evening sunshine. I felt slightly overdressed with the black jacket on, which, in my mind may have been an attempt at a 'cool' appearance but was not conducive to a low body temperature.

Negotiating the entrance to the building, my old friend the merchandise stall greeted me - We exchanged opening glances and formulated a plan to conclude our conversation later. Prince had promised this would be the 'last time' he would play the hits in this setting, and presumably he meant in this arena, as he would perform similar shows in various other venues across the world, and he certainly didn't retire from live performance. Granted, he didn't play the 02 again, but, as it stood, I did look upon this as potentially the last Prince concert I would see...and I wanted to mark it. A programme, CD (NEWS, which I didn't own in original form), book (Prince in Hawaii) and a 'symbol' neck chain were all snapped up, to the tune of roughly 90 pounds - a bargain! I left the T-shirts, as the two designs for men were poor - much more interesting were the female shirts, depicting various retrospective album sleeves, and, in the case of 'Purple Rain' a shot from a slightly different angle that the album cover.

Content with my haul, off we went to enter the concert auditorium - what became very apparent was how modern the whole place was - nothing like my memories of a shabby looking Wembley Arena. A free copy of the 'Planet Earth' CD each and off to look for our seats. As with 'Lovesexy' the stage (shaped as per the infamous 'symbol') was 'in the round' - or as central as it could possibly be. Our seats were on the second level, near one of the mixing desks. This was certainly the largest indoor arena I had been to for a concert and as the lights went down and the intro video started, a familiar emotion came over me - A combination of excitement, anticipation, a touch of fear and a dash of confusion and then, the familiar words 'Dearly beloved, we are gathered here today'. I let out a loud high pitched scream and we were off. There he was, in white, almost angelic in appearance and as cool as ever. I could just make out his features, but not as well as I had been able to do previously - it was, without doubt, him - the way he moved, the way he held his guitar, and, above everything, the way he sang. His voice sounded as rich, solid and versatile as ever. His dance moves were perhaps not as extravagant and flamboyant as back in the day (there were rumours of hip surgery), but he still looked slim and agile as he cavorted around the stage with his dancers 'the twins' and ripped through a set list which was heavy on singles, but also included a number of covers, almost in a revue style. Two of my all-time favourite Prince songs were aired in 'The One' and, almost perfectly, 'If I Was Your Girlfriend' - the very first time I had heard him sing this song live. It was a special moment, more so that my fiancé was next to me. What was abundantly apparent was that Prince had lost none of his ability to hold an audience captive in the palm of his hand - this was, after all, an artist who had not had a Top Ten single in the UK for pushing ten years. He played the band leader, the flirt, the guitar hero and the sensitive lover all in one night - This was Prince the superstar, doing one of the things he did best - play to adoring legions. I was, once again, star stuck and felt truly in the presence of someone on a higher level. The set closed with 'Nothing Compares 2 U' - an absolute triumph.

Outside of the venue, we met up with my sister and talked enthusiastically about what a show it had been. Lorraine and I returned, briefly to our hotel, to leave my souvenirs, and, almost without catching breath, were back for the after show, across the way from the 02 concert hall. After a short, orderly queue, we were inside the venue which was more like a club. On the way in we were asked not to take any photographs or use recording devices. Prince had been extremely particular about this, and, as much as I would have loved to have a personal souvenir, I completely respected his wishes. It becomes increasingly annoying, whilst attending concerts, to see the amount of people standing in the crowd pointing a mobile device at the stage in a bid to capture some grainy imagery, with average sound facilities. Yes, back in the day, it was quite an achievement to track down a poorly recorded video, shot from one angle of a show you had been at, but this has now gone beyond someone wanting to make a few pounds out of fans desire - It's off putting, selfish and very much indicative of 'the cult of me' which has crept into society, since the popularity of mobile phones emerged. Prince (and more so his people) took a dim view of this and expressed preference for concert goers to live in the moment and feel the music. I concurred.

The venue itself was, again, very new, and was decked out in '3121' logos. What made it even more enticing and exciting was that the music being played pre-show had a purple flavour - 'Nasty Girl' and 'the Glamorous Life' bounced out of the speaker and I felt in heaven - I had never thought I would hear these songs played anywhere but my own bedroom or on headphones - certainly not in a 3000 capacity club!

The room was full and the expectation palpable - Prince had made some appearances on stage at the after shows, to even greater reviews than the main arena show, but, as we were all forewarned, it was not a guarantee he would appear. The crowd was buoyant, fuelled by alcohol - myself included, although by now, it was an energy drink that was needed - Seeing Prince once in a night had been one thing, but the prospect of two, going into the small hours of the morning would require a boost! Lorraine too was flagging - we had been on the go, travelling from Newcastle since mid-morning, then across London on a busy tube line. This had paid dividends, but at this point there was a slight lull. Lorraine sat down resting her back against a wall after talking to one of the security staff who disclosed that Prince was definitely in the room. We positioned ourselves to the left of the stage with some room around us. Then without warning the band walked onto the stage and began playing. An instrumental, funky jam, Shelby in the background, almost anticipating an appearance to her right...And then, completely without fanfare, he appeared, almost like a mystical character from a fairy story. Dressed head to toe in black, wearing loose hipster trousers, and a hat, partly covering his features, but unmistakably this was Prince.

I was about five metres away from him, and, yes, I had a moment, but that's all it was. The alcohol fuelled Saturday night crowd broke out into minor scuffles, more so when mobile phones were removed by security staff. Prince played on - not saying a word, head bowed. He was using the same guitar that he had in 'Purple Rain' for 'Let's go Crazy' and 'Computer Blue' and it was there, right in front of me - He was there, playing it. Any lingering alcohol drained out of my body, replaced by a rush of adrenalin. Lorraine recounts the look on my face as joyous shock - A look apparently came over me that she has never seen me express before. But then, almost as soon as he had appeared, he put down his guitar, and calmly walked off stage while the band continued with the remainder of the set. He hadn't appreciated the turn in atmosphere upon his appearance and decided enough was enough for tonight. This was tantalising, but, understandable. There was a forewarning over this, and he had lived up to his sometimes truculent persona. Lorraine confirmed with the security staff - he would not be returning to the stage this evening. We stayed and lapped up the remainder of the band's set, and we left. I have to say I was, at this point, slightly deflated - this was a great night, but it could have been so much better – Or, perhaps I was being greedy. I had observed Prince at close quarters, at an after show party and whilst he hadn't said or sung a word, the experience of being so near to him was unforgettable, as brief as it was.

The next day, Lorraine and I met with my sister and Colin near to where they had been staying and traded experiences of the night before. Taking a mid-afternoon train back to Newcastle, Lorraine and I, somewhat drained, relaxed, with a glass of wine. I played 'NEWS' on my headphones and reflected on the experience with a somewhat heavy heart. The days immediately after the concert were, in all honesty, quite flat. Very much like a perpetual 'first week in January' feeling, I just couldn't raise much enthusiasm. Prince was still in the country, performing shows, to somewhat mixed reviews, depending on who was reviewing and what night it was. One of the 'broadsheet' newspapers ran a piece for every night of the 21, with a different writer each time. I kept all of them. The Prince fan site Prince.org was full of snippets and comments around the shows. In truth, on reflection, I hadn't had the greatest experience, and this was, to some extent, down to my eyesight not being as sharp as it was.

It was very clear that it was Prince I was seeing, but, from a distance, it was very difficult to make out, with clarity, his face and features. I had to squint, which hurt my eyes if I persisted. With the tagline of this being the 'last time' Prince would play the 'hits' and with availability for some nights towards the end of the run, I decided I HAD to go to another. Having made the journey once, I could see how feasible it was and how I didn't NEED to spend a great deal of money to get down. I also felt it was necessary to see Prince with Darran 'one last time' and we talked about the potential dates available.

Again, weekends would be key, and, as it happened the last Sunday performance (September 16th) had some availability. I booked the tickets for the show - they were on the third tier, which was far from ideal, but still, we were going. During a break at work one day in the lead up to the shows while perusing 'tales from the after shows' via the ever informative 'prince.org' I booked tickets for the after show following the show on September 16th - Again, we had secured the hotel next to the arena (I thought), so there were no issues with a late night/early morning public transport rush. This was gaining momentum and was shaping up to be quite an occasion. However, I was still slightly underwhelmed at the ticket location. Yes, Prince would be centre stage, but given that I had struggled with making him out on tier 2 previously, what chance would I have, a whole level higher? I took a gamble. My sister's position, working for the agency which sold the tickets for the show meant that she may be able to switch our tickets - Darran and I would be happy to pay additional costs to secure better seats, if any were available. There were no 'VIP' packages for the gigs, which is very much the norm now - a 'gold circle' ticket gets you front row seats, often the chance to meet the performer and access to 'exclusive' merchandise, all at a premium cost. This hadn't quite kicked in with Prince yet, although it would be something that did become available (as with all other performers) and very much the norm, moving forward.

How she managed it, I don't know, but my sister was able to get us tickets 'on the floor' However, due to time restraints, I would need to collect them from the box office on the day of the performance. This was exciting, but also nervy. I was in a bit of a panic about this, as I had always had tickets with me before going into Prince's shows, or, at least, knew that I was on a reputable coach, where tickets would be distributed en route. I kept this to myself, as I didn't want to alarm Darran. It would surely be ok? I had my sister's numbers with me, and contacts in her department, just in case, although with it being a Sunday show, the chances of someone being available to assist, were limited.

Darran and I took an afternoon train to London (my memory tells me that I met Darran en route, as he travelled from Edinburgh). On the journey down, we chatted, candidly about the prospect of seeing Prince again, together, as we had actually only been seated together once in the past for an evening with our hero. Returning to the 02 area, I was slightly disappointed that all of the posters advertising Prince's shows had all disappeared, to be replaced with the next big act appearing at the arena. It almost felt as if it was an inconvenience that Prince was still here. As the run of shows had progressed, there were a few reports of fatigue, and some shorter 'by numbers' performances in the main hall, with sporadic (yet still sometimes brilliant) club shows afterwards. Had Prince overshot himself here? Would our performance be one of the so called 'lesser' outings? Would this really matter? After all, this was Prince, he was unpredictable, but that was part of his appeal - We bought into this with that knowledge and were quite happy to approach each aspect of his career with the same nervous anticipation and excitement as this.

Two hurdles needed to be overcome before we could guarantee our rite of passage to the show. Firstly, I needed to pick up the tickets. This was internally, for me, a stress - I didn't divulge to Darran how concerned I was about this - It all seemed a huge risk travelling to London to pick up tickets that weren't in my name. Still, as the worst case scenario, we had tickets to the after show, where surely Prince would appear??

After a bit of a nervous exchange of reference numbers and bits of paper at the 02 box office, I was given our tickets to perceptible relief! Notably, the tickets carried a different picture of Prince that the ones I had for the August 4th show. Also, very prominently, the tickets indicated 'floor seats' although the actual position of our seating would not be revealed until later in the evening. I was relieved and felt as if a weight had been lifted. I could now look forward to our next challenge.

We now needed to secure our room for the evening. When the booking was made, there appeared to be some confusion about my name, which I felt was unresolved. Foolishly, rather than clarifying this I let it fester and gnaw away - But hey, what's the worst that could happen now? We sleep rough? Or perhaps, if this was the case, Prince would spot us on his early morning power run (obviously with his guitar at hand), take pity and invite us to spend some time in his luxury hotel while he created a new album, simultaneously cooking us breakfast, wouldn't he? We never got the opportunity to witness Prince's cooking and instrumentation multi-tasking skills, as, again, after some nervy exchanges which initially saw the receptionist say there wasn't a room for us (it appeared the room had been booked under the name 'Mr Geoff'...how I laughed - in relief). We were safely bedded in for the night, with me happily taking the futon that was provided in the room - truth being, I would have been content with sleeping on the floor. Prince's or otherwise! We had a couple of pre-show drinks, to settle us down, and we set off on the short journey to the arena.

The merchandise stall was still present and still talking to me. In fact, so much so that I had planned a significant purchase to mark this auspicious occasion...a tambourine. This drew a gasp from Darran, not least of all due to the cost - ninety pounds! I don't think, at this point, I had spent that much on a piece of Prince memorabilia - record or otherwise. This was very self-indulgent and exceedingly decadent. What on earth was I going to do with a tambourine? Prince was quite renowned for throwing these out to the crowd (or rather playfully passing them around - health and safety could have had him if he projected them into someone's head!!), and they were aesthetically pleasing. They also weren't tat - proper musical instrument tambourines, with the infamous 'symbol' logo in gold against black. This was extravagant and opulent, but I had to have it. The tambourine is still in its original shrink wrap, as new as it was the day I bought it, which answers the question about what I do with it - I look at it.

Given that we were seated on a lower tier to the show this time, our entrance to the arena was at ground level, not up two escalators as had been the case previously. This was when our first gasp of amazement was produced. We got to the top of the back row of seats and were directed to the front row. When we produced our tickets at this point, we had the velvet rope barrier lowered for us, to allow entry onto the floor. We were then escorted to the seats on the floor and handed over to another member of the arena team, who took us directly to our seats for the night. The VERY FRONT ROW, on the floor, just next to the 'dot' part of the symbol stage. This was beyond comprehension - There were only a handful of other seats near us and no one in front. If Prince were to come over to this side of the stage, he would be smack bang in front of us - about two metres away. We stood in disbelief at our fortune. This would be a beautiful night!

I was reminded of this chain of events a few years later, when in the excellent fan documentary 'Springsteen and I', one concert goer recites his experience of being picked out pre-show and been given two tickets by 'anonymous security' to replace the ones he had saved for but were located in an upper tier of the arena (Madison Square Gardens, if memory serves me right). Whilst there is a confused panic about this, given that the originally purchased tickets are taken, there is also an adrenaline rush, as each time the fan gets to the front of a seating block, he is told to go forward to the next one, and ultimately ends up with front row seats. The fan cannot believe his luck. Both Darran and I felt exactly the same. And, whilst Prince had no input on our fortune, my romantic ideal likes to make me think otherwise - This was Prince thanking us for our loyalty, making sure we would get to be close to him and giving us a personal performance, wasn't it? There were certainly points during the performance where it appeared Prince was making direct and deliberate eye contact with us - he couldn't not. There we were shaking our thang in what to us appeared a perfectly reasonable, but exuberant fashion. And, there was Prince responding with smiles and nods directed to us, for certain?

The performance had started off slightly unconventionally. No support act was present (or at least that I can recall), and as the lights went down and the video intro ended, the band - all present apart from the main man kicked into the outstanding track from the 'Planet Earth' album - 'Chelsea Rodgers' - This was a big favourite of ours, so we gave it the full on treatment singing alone, gyrating as best we could in rhythm to the deep bass line. Lead vocals were delivered by Shelby J - an outstanding talent unleashed by Prince as part of his backing band. The fact that Prince didn't present himself during this song, was a bit odd, but it didn't dampen our enthusiasm. It was notable that the few people around us in our micro section weren't doing likewise - we deduced later that as the song was an album track, and, despite that album being given away free pre-concert that not a great deal of the crowd knew it. It didn't stop us. The tempo slowed down following this onslaught and Shelby delivered a cover of 'Misty Blue' where her vocal versatility shone. Prince was still not present at this point, but he was keeping true to his promise of opening each show differently, although we hadn't quite thought he wouldn't present until song four!

'1999' was the first song Prince appeared on stage to, and yes, there he was, frolicking, prowling, suave, majestic as ever, and, at best, 2-3 metres away! We were so close, we could see his skin. How fresh faced he looked and completely untarnished. His high heels covered by the length of his trousers, which settle perfectly just above ground level. Again, just as for the previous show I had been at, he rattled through a lot of hits, and squeezed in a few covers and some album tracks. He played 'The One' which merged into 'Question of U' - he went off stage, which meant moving down a set of stairs in the middle of the 'symbol' - he gyrated along with the Twinz and led the band as always. His ability to work a crowd was palpable, shifting gears into crowd pleasers 'U Got The Look' and 'Kiss'...and then, just as in 1988, he sat at a piano - just in front of where we were, and he played. And how he played - The recollection of the moment in the middle of Wembley Arena where he made a huge audience feel as if they were in a small room, was repeated and this time, I was next to my close friend - we looked at each other throughout this mini-set aghast. 'Insatiable', 'Adore', 'Dear Mr Man', 'Little Red Corvette' and finally, 'Under the Cherry Moon'. Lights down and back he came for a triumphant 'Purple Rain' - Prince must have played this song hundreds of times, yet each performance I saw appeared as emotional and moving as any other – tonight was no exception. He gave everything - and so did we. The sound may have been a bit 'muddy' at times but it didn't dampen our admiration for the performer. Prince has always seemed relatively candid on stage, happy to talk to thousands where he appeared reticent in front of a microphone and an interviewer off stage.

The encore of 'Nothing compares 2 U' was followed by another 'Prince solo' - This time the oft referred to 'sampler set' where Prince reprises the 'piano' setting, but with a box of tricks containing drum patterns and programmed beats from his better known songs. Slightly teasingly and mischievously, he would often play a few bars of a song intro, then cut it short - he did this with the beginning to 'Darling Nikki' - the song that had caused outrage in the 80's due to the line 'I met her in a hotel lobby masturbating with a magazine' - hardly 'Let's Pretend We're married' but still, not 'remember you're a Womble' either! Prince had distanced himself from playing such suggestive material, following his conversion to the Jehovah's Witnesses. Tonight, was no exception. He played a few bars, to rapturous cheers, but cut the track short - very short - jumping up off his seat wagging his finger, shaking his head and playing up to the anticipating, drooling crowd, to a tee!

Prince ended his sampler set and the show with an edited 'Raspberry Beret' - and he was gone. We left the arena in a strange state of euphoria and slight disorientation - We knew we had just had the experience of our lives, being so close (almost within touching distance) of our hero - He had lived up to all our expectations and cut the consummate rock/pop god with ease. Yes, the set was heavy on 'hits' but that's what we expected - There were also some lesser known tracks and the sections of the show where it felt like he was playing to 'us' were sublime. As euphoria dipped slightly into fatigue, we headed back to the hotel - an energy drink was in order, as there was still the prospect of the after show. And of course, I had my tambourine to safely drop off!

I can't imagine that I would ever contemplate attending an after show performance for anyone other than Prince - The excitement generated from a big show, or in fact any show from a spectator's point of view, when the performer is someone so ingrained into your life, such as Prince, is quite tiring, once the buzz wears off - and this can take some time. Once again we had travelled down on the day of the show (Darran from Edinburgh) - food wasn't high on our agenda, so, with just alcohol and endorphins to fuel us, it's no surprise we flagged a bit just before midnight - both closer to 40 than not, and we were not in the best shape of our lives - despite my attempts to push my fitness regime pre summer!

We arrived back at the 02 and headed for Indigo2. Once we got inside we cased the joint and noticed Shelby standing at the bar area, casual as you like. I contemplated speaking to her and thanking her for the show, but ultimately thought better of it. I may have been brimming with enthusiasm, but I didn't want to make a fool of myself. Eventually, we positioned ourselves towards the back of the stage, centrally positioned. I could just about make the stage out. Around 1am there was some commotion, a rush to the stage and the beginning of a drum and bass beat. The curtain in front of the stage came down to reveal the band, with Prince dead centre. I could visualise him, but only just (a recurring theme at standing gigs for me) - toward the end of the jam like song which was a cover of a Sly Stone number, I mentioned to Darran that it might be better to move, over to stage left, where we wouldn't be so central, but there was a bit of a gap in the crowd. This would pay dividends, later in the set.

In complete contrast to the tight, hit filled, well-choreographed show we had witnessed across the way in the arena, this was had a much more fluid feel with extended (presumed) impromptu jam interludes and Prince seeming more at ease and happy to be in the foreground a lot less - almost a bit player in his own backing band. This was how I'd imagined an after show, and, ok, so it wasn't as sporadic as turning up unannounced, but forget about it this was Prince, in close quarters, showing off all his musical chops, not even two and a half hours after we had seen him in concert! Seeing one Prince Performance in 24 hours was something, but now, we were taken somewhere else, on a different ride, by a different version of Prince. His ability to character (and performance) shift in the space of one night and unleash two contrasting, but equally electric sets in the space of a few hours is testament of not only his unquestionable talent and desire, but also physical stamina. This was 1am in the morning and whist adrenalin kept me going - surely, having done this time after time, it would take its toll on him? Luckily not tonight - and I genuinely mean that - there was a huge element of fortune was with us - the fact that he was playing at the after show in itself was an achievement - that he played one of the more varied sets, was incredible. The set included reworkings of several older songs (Girls and Boys and Gotta Broken Heart) and much more expansive versions of others - the groove to '3121' knocked the already memorable album track into another stratosphere.

Very much in a playful mode and content to throw out comments - he told a tale about a photographer's desire to capture an image of him and Michael Jackson 'if I could just get the shot, I could retire' and then went into a bluesy comedic routine about a 'three handed woman' who, we were told was 'left handed, right handed and underhanded' This was all an incredible experience, the things that dreams are made of, and yet, more was to follow. Another Sly Stone cover (Everyday People) turned towards a familiar extended jam workout, where fans at the very front of the crowd were being invited up onto the stage - This was going to be me, which I muttered to Darran and began moving forward. I got no nearer the stage than perhaps two steps and thought better of it. I moved back to our 'spot' just in front of the bar, stage left, recognising that I could no longer see Prince - Presumably he had gone off stage for an outfit change, although I thought I could still hear his guitar and the vocal refrain 'liaayyye am everyday people..' led by Shelby.

I continued to groove when, out of nowhere, I was grabbed and pulled by my shirt with a shriek from Darran - 'Geoff, it's Prince' - I spun around and there he was - barely a metre away from me strumming his guitar - all in black, wearing a hat and looking cool as f*ck - I played it cool and continued to gyrate - there were about 10 people, seemingly gathered in a circle around him, and Shelby who held the mic out for Darran to provide vocals. This could not be happening, could it? Had he picked us out? Was this the reason I had gravitated to this spot in the room? After a few seconds stationary, Prince and Shelby were on the move and strolled in their cool demeanour toward a lift that would take them to the upper floor of the venue. Prince turned round and laid his back against the lift wall - STILL playing guitar - I attempted to get in and carry on with the adventure, only to be politely, yet abruptly stopped by a burly looking security fella 'that's as far as you go mate'...this is when the reality of what happened kicked in - Prince was standing in front of ME (okay and some others) about a metre/metre and a half away playing guitar, while my longest friend did backing vocals for him...WOW! Prince passed us again briefly on his way back to the stage, but this happened so quickly, coupled with the high security presence that it was just a glimpse - He got back to the stage area via the same side door that he had presumably come out of - just metres away from our 'spot'. This was the greatest single experience of my life to date - and Darran was there with me all the way.

The show ended, sometime close to 3am and we stood around, in disbelief chatting to other fortunate souls around us - I was clearly noticeably overcome and there was a comment passed to me in an obviously London accent 'yeah mate, that did fahkin happen?' Thinking back, I can only describe 'that' moment as utter unfounded and uncontrollable elation. Was this the pinnacle? It was, but there would be a notable footnote - the whole after show was being recorded (I guess all of them were), which may explain the performance Prince pulled, although the idealist in me thinks it was because Darran and I were present. Prince would release a glossy hardback book of the whole run at the 02 with photos by Randy St Nichol '21 nights' was a heavyweight publication, very much like an extended tour programme, with a few 'candid' shots presenting, in the main, contrived pictures. Contained in the book was an accompanying CD, with live tracks recorded at two after shows - one of which was the 16th/17th September 2007. The track 'Girls and Boys' from the show was included which had Prince encourage the crowd to sing backing - which we all did. I still visualise the majority of fans mimicking the hand motions Prince did in the promo video while chanting 'Vous etre belle, mama, Girls and Boys' - and there it is, I (and Darran) recorded with Prince...go on, indulge me on this, please!

Prince had claimed this would be his last visit to the UK to perform his 'hits' - If this was to be the case, I was more than content with my experiences of seeing him live – seven concerts, two after shows and a bag full of memories and experiences on a level far higher than anything I had witnessed in live music EVER. I couldn't ask for anything more and a huge part of me didn't want Prince to return - What could possibly top this?

Prince did return (don't they all?)- he played the 'HOP' festival in 2008, but it didn't really make it onto my agenda. There was also a performance scheduled for Croke Park in Dublin, which was a serious consideration. Luckily, we didn't book for this, as the date was pulled AFTER tickets had gone on sale (shades of Wembley 87), so maybe the 02 was to be the last we would see of Prince live in the UK...Or, was it?

The year 2014 would be quite a momentous one in my life, and very much like the majority of life experiences, very little of it was planned. In terms of 'my life with Prince' there had been no UK tours since the '21 nights' run. Sporadic shows occurred, but very few (if any) on these shores. There had been output - 2009 saw a triple CD set containing two new Prince albums 'Lotus Flower' and 'Minneapolis Sound', as well as the debut from current protégé Bria Valete. Released initially as a download via the latest incarnation of the NPG music club, which this time I joined (if for nothing else than to get the exclusive T-shirt!), the albums were a mixed bag - Prince simultaneously moving forward and adopting a retro sound, with the reintroduction of the Linn drum on many of the more dance based 'Minneapolis Sound' tracks. The stand out tune across the set, was easily 'Colonised Mind' - a guitar driven, momentum building mid pacer. This showed that Prince could still cut the axe hero, as he had done on say 'The Cross' in the past.

Obtaining the physical album on day of release was to be challenging. Prince had initially agreed an exclusive distribution deal with US store 'Target'. There were no branches in the UK. A stroke of luck bestowed upon me (again, was it Prince's guidance and oversight that made this happen?) whereby Lorraine was taking her annual trip to Las Vegas, and, whilst there wasn't a 'Target' store on the Las Vegas 'strip', Lorraine did locate one, slightly out of town and picked up two copies (one for Darran). By this point in our relationship, Lorraine and I had been together 9 years, and Lorraine was fully on board with the importance Prince played in my life, and how frustrated I would be not to get my hands on the CD. I received a text message confirming the purchase and I was quite thrilled. At the same time, I had downloaded the set and noticed that there was a slight variation in the track listing with 'Forever' being a download exclusive...cunning.

Prince played a few European shows late in 2009, and there was, I thought, an opportunity to see him in Paris where Lorraine and I were taking a mini break. It didn't work out - I seem to recall he arrived a week after we left, but I was able to obtain a single CD of 'Minneapolis Sound' on the trip, which I hadn't seen up to that point - There was always time to pick up a Prince rarity on holiday!

2010 saw Prince release '2010' - another 'cover mount' with a UK national newspaper - this time one of the 'red tops' - Again, a big coincidence in that I was in hospital undergoing some corrective surgery on my wrist when Prince was receiving daily coverage in the UK press, which was attempting to maximise its weekend sales (when the album would be given away) by carrying profiles and interviews (and pictures) in the run up to the CD distribution. In truth, the album wasn't Prince's best, despite the proclamations within the newspaper telling me otherwise. It seemed that each time Prince released an album it was hailed as a 'return to form' or his 'best since 'Sign 'O' the times" - I don't think, realistically this was ever going to be the case, and I honestly don't think Prince ever thought along those lines - His view was, pretty much, always to move forward. He may not have released a stunningly consistent challenging, genre busting set, but was he ever going to? Could anyone?

Prince always had gems on his albums and was perfectly adept at producing radio friendly 'hits' - none more so than 2012's 'Rock n Roll Love Affair' which received a large amount of airplay on UK radio stations (although probably not prime time 'Radio 1' as was the case in the 80's). Hearing a new Prince track on the radio so frequently was a turn up, and a joy to behold - made even more special as it was around the Christmas period. I snapped up the single in as many formats as possible, noting the cover contained Prince with a tight 'fro' hairstyle, and that the record was released via 'Purple Music' - Prince seemed to be a record label tourist, signing short term deals with one album (or one single!) being the agreement. Notably, the single was available on 12-inch vinyl and picture disc, although it was easier to obtain both of these via mail order via the Internet. Over the next couple of years, Prince would release more great tracks and some average ones via downloads only - His latest web project 'Third eye tunes' was the platform for this, with some tracks finding their way onto ITunes, the biggest online download store on the market. There were rumours of an album in the pipeline 'Plectrumelectrum' and he had a new band, the all-female '3rdeyegirl'. It was also approaching the 30th year anniversary of the release of 'Purple Rain' and there was clamour for this to be acknowledged with a release of a remastered version of the album, containing outtakes and B-sides.

2014 was shaping up to be quite a year of activity for Prince. It would be quite a busy year for me too. Lorraine and I had been together 13 years in 2013, and we had settled into our new home, which, although still with issues to overcome, was a step up from our previous house. Late in 2013 I had a small health scare in that I was unable to swallow and digest food properly - My doctor arranged for me to have an investigation, which was moved forward somewhat hurriedly. Working in the health service, I know that if a test is arranged at such pace, there is, generally a suspicion of cancer and the test is required to be performed within a set timeframe in order to either rule out a tumour, or, if it is a worst case scenario to commence treatment. I was very worried about this, although tried not to let it show. As it turned out, there wasn't anything sinister, so I could put all my concerns over this away. It did, however make me think and reflect, particularly about my relationship with Lorraine. We had been together for over a decade but had nothing legal to confirm our status. We had a joint bank account and jointly owned our house, but little else.

As it happens, Lorraine was clearly thinking along similar grounds, as on New Year's Eve as we were sitting at home, drinking and waiting for the year to turn over, contemplating our ambitions for the year ahead. Lorraine said she thought we should get married. I agreed without hesitation. We had been happily engaged since 2006 and hadn't had any firm plans to become man and wife, largely due to the fact that neither of us especially liked the thought of the attention a ceremony would bring. What would be key for this was a venue and the guest list. We wanted it just to be our immediate family, and we wanted to hold the event and 'after show' at the same venue. Initially, Lorraine thought of Las Vegas. I thought of Gretna Green. We came to a joint decision that it should really be in Newcastle and after some thought, discussion and selection, went for the Laing Art Gallery, a venue we both enjoyed visiting and had spent many an afternoon there together, admiring artwork. The big draw was that we would be wed in front of our favourite paintings.

Music would play a vital part in the day, and I soon began to compile three different 'setlists' there would be an 'intro' of relaxed instrumentals, played pre ceremony when I and the guests awaited the bridal party. There would be the music for the ceremony, followed by the music for the 'wedding breakfast'. Like the majority of the wedding arrangements, where we took a 'hands on' approach between us, I would put the music together myself. I wasn't trusting this to anyone. I was galvanised in putting the selections together and knew right from the start that Prince would feature heavily throughout. Lorraine appreciated Prince, and also acknowledged how highly I valued him as a musical idol. So much so, in fact, that she bought me a pair of 'Symbol' cufflinks as a wedding gift, which I discovered on the morning of our wedding. I also managed to acknowledge Prince in my wedding speech with the closing line 'I never meant to cause you any sorrow, I never meant to cause you any pain, I only wanted to make you happy, I only wanted to marry you Lorraine'. It received a mild appreciation. Lorraine has always accepted my love for Prince, and my fervour to collect product and memorabilia.

There has, very often been a Prince related story to holidays and trips away we have enjoyed together, completely unplanned, but equally not dismissed by Lorraine - such as the time we holidayed in Las Vegas and I discovered a Prince tribute act playing in one of the hotels bars - of course we went, twice, the first time I got extremely carried away (assisted by alcohol) and found myself dancing along to 'D.M.S.R' and, more so, the set the 'fake' Time did. There was the occasion we attended a country music festival at the O2 (familiar venue??) to see one of Lorraine's favourite artists, Darius Rucker. Darius played a very solid set, more to Lorraine's taste than mine, but I enjoyed the experience. For his last song, Darius announced that the song he would close with would be a cover, and if it worked, it was his idea, if it didn't, it would be the guitarists. I thought the tempo and slow melody to this song were familiar, but dismissed my initial thoughts, until it became too obvious. It was 'Purple Rain' - how ironic that it should be played in the 02 arena. Lorraine just can't escape Prince! As a footnote to the wedding, on the day of the ceremony, when I was not staying in the house, there was a delivery for me, which on the mailing label had 'from Prince'. This was quite astounding - he hadn't made it to the day, but he was sending me a gift? He did care! It turned out to be two limited edition mugs I had ordered from the 3rdeyetunes store, which arrived on September 20th, the day we got married. A happy coincidence, or not? Our wedding day was (and still is) the best day of my life, and in 2014, I also experienced the best concert of my life

Very early in 2014, there was news from Prince. Unexpected and exciting news too - he was to play shows in the UK, during February, utilising smaller clubs/ concert halls. No more details were revealed, but I had had a minor insight into the sort of venues he may play, when during a visit to an art exhibition of rare rock photographs, one of the curators mentioned that a venue in Newcastle had been looked over for a potential performance. This, unfortunately didn't come off, but it did set me off relishing the potential opportunity of seeing Prince again in a small venue. I followed updates on the internet daily and counted down the days to February. The shows would be part of his 'Hit and run' shows with 3rdeyegirl and would see him play London dates, which would be announced on the day, with no presale, and tickets 'on the door' so to speak. Not, ideally what I wanted to hear, and, despite the early reviews of shows at Camden Electric Ballroom, which were more than positive, it was something that ultimately, I just couldn't get to. I could possibly get two days off work at short notice, and travel to London and hope on one of those days a gig would be announced and then hope I got in, but it was all ifs buts, maybes - a lot of conjecture. I just couldn't put my life on hold for Prince. As a birthday present, Lorraine offered to pay for travel and accommodation for a couple of nights in the capital, but, as sweet and generous an offer as this was, I just couldn't sanction using the amount of money against the possibility of not getting to a show. I'd rather not attempt it as the risk factors were high and I would be, quite frankly, angry, if either I hadn't got into a show, or there was a show announced as I was returning home. Darran felt the same way - he would need to travel from Edinburgh and simply could not justify the outgoing on something that had a high chance of not happening.

Then things changed, and it was actually on my birthday that events began to fall in our favour, although I didn't know it at the time. Prince was playing a show in a tiny venue for journalists and invited guests (some fans also got in, as I recall) in London on February 14th. During that performance, he announced that he would be playing some shows in Manchester, the following weekend. I read this news on February 15th, slightly hungover and with a rush of adrenalin, thought 'this becomes doable' I talked it over with Lorraine, and formulated my plan - If we got to Manchester, we could hang around, ready to move to the venue. My sister, Margaret, by this point worked in Manchester so would have a better oversight of the area and venues. My sister also still worked in the event ticketing field and may be able to find out information with a little advance warning. This gained momentum very quickly and by Tuesday a venue was announced, and our plan would be to arrive there as early as possible on the Saturday morning and queue. Darran planned to get an overnight bus from Edinburgh, and I would drive to Liverpool, where my sister lived with her husband and where we would stay the night after the gig - should we get in. Prince was the hottest ticket in town, a true reflection of how he had transcended generations and still maintained relevance, 30 years after his big breakthrough. As a matter of fact, my friend and host of the Record Player, Steve Drayton was keen on airing the Purple Rain film in a special event and Steve and I actually went to Whitley Bay the Tuesday before I travelled to Manchester to talk to the organisers of the annual film festival there, with the aim of showing the film that summer. Unfortunately, it didn't happen here, but this didn't dampen enthusiasm to get the film on the big screen in the North East at some point this year.

Wednesday February 19th - Prince was appearing on The Brits to present an award. Tickets for the Manchester shows were to go on sale - confirmed were two shows, and it was possible more would follow. As we were going to stay in Liverpool, my sister was keen to make the short trip to Manchester from Liverpool and see Prince in close quarters. Margaret had been a fan by proxy, as countless repeated airings of his catalogue was clearly heard by her in our time living at our parent's house - despite her favouring Michael Jackson in the 80's! In fact, Margaret had actually seen Michael Jackson in concert in 1988 - the same year I first saw Prince - Quite an achievement for us both to see our musical idols at the peak of their powers whilst we were both in our teens!

Margaret was confident that she would be able to get the four tickets, which was the maximum permitted - sales were via the Internet only, and it would, obviously be first come, first served. Margaret was actually travelling back from London that evening having given a presentation, which was quite nerve wracking - In her own words, it wasn't nearly as nerve wracking as trying to get the purchase of the tickets through, given her laptop was running on very low battery! Just as Prince came on stage at the Brits, the tickets went on sale - Friday first, which I was able to see online - frantically text messaging Margaret to make sure she could log in etc. Then Saturdays went on sale, just minutes later, as it seemed Fridays had sold out. A nervous wait. As Prince was presenting the award and looking damn cool, with extra swagger, news came through from Margaret - she had them! Unbelievable! We wouldn't need to stand in line or count numbers of people, nervously working out if we would get in (although I had read that it was all relatively good humoured and civil in these queues for the gigs). The excitement over this was unprecedented. I phoned Darran, who tried to remain calm, but failed. We made travel plans - He would come down to Newcastle on Friday, stay at his parents, and come to mine early Saturday morning where I would drive to Liverpool, with Margaret ultimately driving to Manchester. Just over a week ago, I was in the doldrums - the prospect of not seeing Prince when he was in the UK had been a hard burden to carry. He didn't visit the UK often and the shows were getting some of the best reviews of his career. Footage posted on his website confirmed that Prince was surpassing himself at the moment, and it seemed like a plan for another crack at world domination was imminent - A new deal with Warner's, which would see the label promote all future releases and regain control of his back catalogue was imminent - timely with 'Purple Rain' hitting 30. Prince also had an abundance of new tracks - some of which he was playing at the current shows, in a bid to give greater exposure to the 3rdeyegirl album 'Plectrumelectrum' which seemed to have been in the making for a number of years. He also had an appearance on US comedy show 'New Girl' which saw him send himself up brilliantly. There wasn't a better time to be a Prince fan, and that feeling just got better - We were in possession of the most sought after ticket in entertainment at that time, and it had all fallen into place perfectly.

The nights leading up to the shows were restless ones - 'Two more sleeps to Prince', then 'one more sleep to Prince', then none. Truth was I didn't sleep much, and I had almost pushed myself into a frenzy by the time Friday came. So, as I could make use of our car at the weekend, Lorraine took her mother shopping on the Friday night, while I did the weekly housework, throwing down some 'moves' to the Prince music I had playing via my headphones. This time tomorrow, I would be there, outside the venue...nearly there.

As planned, Darran arrived, at our house on Saturday morning, dropped off by his parents and we set off, with me driving to Liverpool. We made very good time and enjoyed chatting and listening to CDs (not exclusively Prince flavoured). Prince had, seemingly played a great set the previous night, but there was some controversy over a proposed spontaneous second show, hours later, which hadn't taken place, despite fans queuing and being told a second show would happen. Alarm set in. Would Prince show his sometimes truculent side, decide that this negative media coverage was unjustified and pack his bags? This was the last show scheduled for the run - He said he would be here 'in February' and it looked like this would be it, having decanted north. It was not going to be straightforward, despite us having tickets (although the tickets actually were nothing more than print outs from PDF files - nothing like the lavish efforts from the 02).

After an afternoon at Margaret and Colin's house in Liverpool, while they were both at work, we set off for Manchester with Margaret driving, stopping off to pick up the fourth concert goer, Margaret's friend, Beth. We arrived at Manchester and stood in line at the venue, the doors opening at 7pm. As it was February in the North of England, it was cold. Very cold. But this would all be worth it, as we would warm up inside. As we go closer to the door, Margaret distributed the print out tickets, which we received with glee. I looked over the ticket and did a double take - the date showing was February 21st - that was yesterday? I pointed this out as calmly as I could to Margaret - she looked panic stricken. She was adamant she had booked for the Saturday, and had the receipt on an email, via her portable device - We would be ok, wouldn't we?? My suggestion was to keep calm, say nothing and just hope we got through with no problem. Under no circumstances should we draw attention to our plight. Margaret would be able to talk to the event duty manager if we didn't get in first hand. We didn't get in - The tickets were required to be read by an electronic scanner - the scanner didn't read our codes. We were taken to one side and Margaret had some discussion over the booking. Slightly more complicated was the fact that the tickets had been booked with a credit card which didn't match the mail account, as Margaret was using an old email address in her maiden name. I said nothing, but contemplated not getting in and also just rushing the door in a mad frenzy. No need for this - after some protracted negotiation, we were good. I asked to maintain one of the tickets as a keepsake, despite the date error. We got into the hall and breathed a massive collective sigh of relief... Alcohol was needed! I was quite keen not to overindulge on drink, for many reasons, least of all as I didn't want to miss any of the performance - It was a standing venue, and likely to be quite cramped, so I was happy with one drink. I was also planning on driving back to Newcastle that night, so it was wise not to have more alcohol than was legal. The hall was, quite basic - very much in the 'University' type mould, no real frills and not somewhere I would have ever imagined Prince playing. We took position, not right at the front, but near enough, to the left, just as we were for the Indigo2 - We couldn't be that lucky again, could we? There were no plans to move - The heat generated from the crowd diluted any need to use the lavatories, which was just as well.

The anticipation grew and grew, until, almost on 8pm, the house lights went down, plunging us into ecstatic and frenzied cheers. He spoke, introducing the show ('Manchester, are you ready'?) - heavy, drawn out drum beats and then '1, 2, 3'... A familiar riff, but somewhat slower - a new take on 'Let's Go Crazy', up came the lights - and there he was, majestic, with his guitar, wearing tinted glasses and sporting a larger than life 'fro', reminiscent of the 'For You' period. '..if you don't like...the world you're living in'...delivered now in a street smart blues-esque drawl, the guitar still the driving force, but now free of keyboard backing, Prince could let his lead take the track where he desired, having abandoned the previous frenzied structure of the song. Despite this version being known by only few in attendance, the crowd all sang along, in time, when needed and participated in some choreographed cheering, at Prince's bequest.

Lots of breaks in lyric delivery, allowed Prince to maximise soloing in front of the adoring crowd I was transfixed - just I had been in 88, 90, 93, 95 and 2007 - This was Prince in close quarters, playing a 'sweaty' gig - not a theatrical arena show, or jam based after show - a fully-fledged 'gig'. You couldn't tell the difference, as he was as energetic and engaging as ever. The sound was much clearer and, despite there being crowd movement, it was, initially, not difficult to see him. He strutted around the stage, prowling, preening and pulling numerous 'Prince' faces. 'Let's Go Crazy (reloaded)' ended with a masterclass in guitar soloing - fast paced, part improvised, part self-indulgent (permitted when you have this amount of Princely goodness about you), he went from the end 'Let's Go Crazy' solo into the high tempo bouncer 'Guitar' - determined to allow the band 3rdeyegirl as much limelight, they all also soloed, showing off their musical chops - Prince appeared to be relishing being the lead guitarist, but very keen to do a joint solo with Donna or Ida. Hannah on drums was equally not to be left out. Darran and I looked at each other with contented astonishment -

Once again, this was happening in our Prince life - We were being taken to a higher level by his incomparable brilliance.

As the set developed, it became very clear, very early on that Prince was in the mood of his life tonight - What bliss it was to see and hear him play full extended versions of the reworked 'Something in the Water' and 'She's Always In My Hair' - even the recent tracks that hadn't sounded wonderful on release were given a new dimension - 'Fixurlifeup' became 3D and new track 'Plectrumelectrum' was hard rock in a funky place for sure. It was very difficult to keep up with the pace of the show and where Prince would go next, extracting something from just about every era of career, from the tender 'when we're dancing close and slow' to some high highlights from Sign O the Times - including the title track in full and a rasping 'Hot Thing'. So, engrossed in the moment, I even took it upon myself to politely confront a taller youth standing in front of me and seemingly intent on doing nothing more than talking to his (presumed) girlfriend. Periodically, this was blocking my view of the show, so riding on the crest of euphoria, I seized my chance when his partner moved off to get a drink. Ultimately this would be fruitful but proved hard work - The bloke wanting to keep enough space around him, so he could dance easily. This was a new one on me, and after pointing out he was taller than me and there was enough Prince for all, he reluctantly concurred and permitted me to stand in front of him. I felt vindicated, as after a further 20 mins they both left. Fools. Back to the concert experience of my life and Prince seemed hell bent on giving the crowd every conceivable song they wanted...Well, it certainly felt that way. 'I Would Die 4 U', a storming 'Housequake', which saw a large portion of the crowd replicate the arm movement as per the 'Sign O the Times' film.

There was one moment, above all when, amongst all of this, I stood aghast - during a cover of the Times' 777-9311. Prince, seemingly spontaneously picked up a bass and began picking away at the tune, looking as comfortable as he did on piano or lead - This was Prince the multi-instrumental musical genius - something I had not witnessed on this scale before - Prince the showman, yes. Prince the arena star, yes. But this - this soared beyond anything I had witnessed anywhere before - who said there wasn't an element of theatre tonight? We were only half way through the performance and I felt I needed a breather - It seemed inhuman for Prince to be putting this amount of energy into the show. He appeared to be bouncing off the crowd, who, in turn were rebounding of him, forming a symbiotic circle of electricity all juiced by track after track from Prince's extensive and exquisite career - I don't think I have ever experienced an artist so at ease and in the zone as Prince was - He held the crowd and controlled it with his music and direction, having some fans on stage, although they were kept at a safe distance. There were times, especially when he sported an eye mask, (thus flattening his fro), when he appeared to look like the Prince from 1984 in Purple Rain, with his clothing (inappropriately or not) resembling his wardrobe from that period. My body felt as if it was lifted to another point in time, momentarily giving me a glimpse of how Prince was in this period of his career, concurrently recognising that he was just as hot, if not hotter now, 30 years later.

The song 'Purple Rain' featured in a soothing piano driven version, another first for me in hearing it played this way - turning me to speculate over the way the song was initially conceived (as hinted at in the film). The song didn't need the aching guitar for its emotional impact to be understood and appreciated.

In what I thought was the slowing down towards the end of the set, Prince left the stage, only to return for the first encore of 'Screwdriver' and 'Chaos and Disorder' - two relatively obscure tracks, which it seemed only Darran and I knew, given our elated response. We may have been physically and emotionally drained, but each time he hit us with another unexpected and outstanding track, we were energised. 'Nothing Compares 2 U' closed the encore, and, somewhat over satisfied I assumed the set would close here - He had done two hours, and there was potentially a second show to play. I was happy to let someone else see Prince tonight, although I'm not quite sure how I would have reacted if there were a second show and I had been offered a ticket. No time to contemplate this - he was back, for the second in a total of five encores - Five fucking encores!!! Who does that? The returns to stage lasted over an hour and he covered even more ground 'The Max', 'Endorphinmachine', 'Bambi' and another Time track 'Cool' which turned into an extended funk workout. A sprinkling of keyboard wizardry with 'Raspberry Beret' and 'Take Me With U' and a smattering of covers - Was there anything he could not turn his hand to? After over three hours (it was now after 11 o'clock) the lights came up, but it wasn't actually over, 'Pretzelbodylogic' (the current 3rdeyegirl single) played out over the P.A. while the band (minus Prince) shook hands with fans at the front of stage. 'We're gonna go away, put the album out and come back soon' said Prince in his parting shot - Part of me kinda didn't want him to - He could never top this - NEVER. I could never top this. It could not get more perfect a show than I had just witnessed. Outside people looked stunned - This was certainly my overriding feeling. I had lost my voice, I was fatigued, I was euphoric, and I was absolutely taken aback at the level of performance from the artist of my life. This showed me that even in my early forties there are still experiences that can be beyond me - I had thought I'd achieved my Prince 'moment' at Indigo2 in 2007, and, indeed at this ripe old age that I'd seen pretty much everything a gig experience could offer Wrong. Prince had demonstrated, once again that it was always possible to achieve the unexpected, to experience new dimensions in life - often when least expecting them.

Despite the show being four years ago, I still have extremely vivid memories of the night - aided, it has to be said by the Internet and the bootleg CD of the evening I have acquired. There are however, moments, even now, when I can, almost unfathomably transport myself, in my mind's eye to that show - the sight lines, the stage, the crowd, the genius that was burning at a febrile temperature that night. I was fortunate in 2014 - Prince played an almost unfathomable gig in front of me, six months before my wedding - his gift to me, and it was the gift that just feels like it kept on giving. Many times over the passing years, I think back to both of these events, which were the two greatest experiences of my life - six months apart, and conclude that for times such as these, you need to go through heartache, pain, and the monotonous humdrum of everyday life, which, for most of us (me included) constitute doing a job that does not inspire at all, yet it becomes a necessity to pay for the good things in life - the holidays with my wife, the house we live in, the wedding we both dreamed of, (and got), and, alongside those, the exploits with your heroes - whoever or whatever they are, the times that make life worth living. February 22nd, 2014 was one of those days.

Driving back from Liverpool the following day, Darran and I were still cruising on cloud 9 (so much so that I was caught driving marginally over the speed limit). We re-lived our experience and tried to pick out highlights, if that were possible. Certainly, Prince picking up the bass during '777-9311' was there, as was the rarer heard guitar driven tracks, and the moment the crowd joined in with the 'Housequake' moves. I got back home, beaming and tried to put the experience into words to Lorraine - I came very close to tears of joy at this point. I think the feeling of pure elation did not leave me for a good two weeks - Yes, I was back at work, and yes, there was still a lot of preparation for the wedding (we had, at this stage, only really begun our visions for the day), but I felt inspired and galvanised and ready to tackle life with a different perspective - It was almost an epiphany. Above everything Prince introduced into my life - this is where I will miss him most, the inspirational live performances. Darran and I, after some weeks, did conclude that if we never saw Prince again, we could be content with the performances we had witnessed, and there is clearly credence to this. Yes, we both wanted more but there are many who didn't see him, and I feel eternally grateful that we were fortunate NOT to be amongst them.

In closing his set at the Manchester Academy, Prince had said he'd be back soon...But they all say that, don't they? 'Soon' is a very open ended timespan, and often means years later. However, on this occasion, Prince was true to his word and in April 2014, it was announced he and 3rdeyegirl would return to the UK in May to perform some arena shows on the 'Hit n Run II' tour. After some discussion and contemplation, I decided I couldn't attend any of these shows - they fell directly after a small operation on my knee, where for a period afterwards, I would be unstable, and likely in pain, and not to mention absent from work for nearly three weeks. This was quite difficult - I needed to have the surgery now to a) cure my pain and b) be fit enough for our wedding. Venues were much closer by (Leeds and Glasgow) and it was extremely tempting to throw caution to the wind, and just go. However, on this occasion, common sense prevailed, and I didn't try for tickets. It was difficult to read the reviews and compare setlists, knowing I was missing out. I consoled myself with the knowledge that the gig at the Academy in Manchester could not be topped and that the intimacy could not be replicated at arena shows.

2014 was the year that just kept on giving. A week prior to our wedding, a new venture by the congenial and affable Steve (Mr) Drayton was launched at the local arthouse cinema - it was a combination of food and a music related film, presented at the Tyneside Cinema 'Mr Drayton's Music and Munchies' would feature the 'Purple Rain' film as its opener. Mr Drayton (Steve) kindly asked me to contribute to the evening, where there was 1984 Prince related music, a quiz and a few facts about the film, which may or may not have been known to the sell-out audience. The evening was a huge success and gave me the opportunity to see the film on the big (ish) screen for the first time. That this came just nine days before our wedding was immaculate timing. The following week would be Mark's 50th birthday, followed on the Saturday by mine and Lorraine's big day. 2014 also saw me attend gigs by the Pet Shop Boys, Adam Ant, Kate Bush and Darius Rucker, amongst others. Our wedding ceremony aside, nothing would top seeing Prince live that year.

Looking back now and realising 2014 was the last time I would ever see Prince, there is a mixture of emotions that run through me. I'm very proud that Darran and I achieved the almost impossible in seeing him at close quarters and still get a rush thinking about the night in 2014, which, thankfully is extremely vivid in my mind's eye. But, as with any passing, knowing you will never be in the presence of that person again, hurts, deeply. Prince's music will live on and on, and he may well have a further renaissance, gaining new fans, in the way that I have become a fan of artists such as The Doors, or Jimi Hendrix, who were before my time. However, it is a huge sadness which overwhelms me knowing that the experience of being at a Prince concert cannot be lived again, for anyone. Going to a Prince concert was the ultimate Holy Grail for me - the fact that I achieved it (and then some!!) does, at times, make me take a step back, think about where it all started, my background, and what I have achieved in pop music fandom. If I'm totally honest, whilst I still attend gigs/concerts, there is part of me that feels I am going through the motions. I'll never go to a Prince show again, and that hurts. Granted, the recordings preserve some of his performances, but his presence and electricity and shear star aura cannot be captured in this medium. I'm thankful for the moments I had, regretful that there weren't more.

As a matter of fact, there was one last opportunity to experience Prince live in the UK, and, very much like the 'Hit n Run' shows it came out of nowhere and led to a frenzied few days in terms of planning tickets and travel, given that the shows would take place weeks before Christmas, in late November/early December 2015, and would only go on sale on November 12th. The 'Piano and a microphone' shows would be exactly that - Prince, unaccompanied, solo, focused, intimate, playing his songs as many of them had originated - via his piano. He would play two shows each night, and, it seemed Glasgow, being on a Friday night would be Darran's and my preferred choice. Ticket prices were not cheap, but this didn't really enter my consciousness. I took the 12th November as a day's leave, which would be the best thing to do, given I would utilise phone and Internet purchasing opportunities. I hadn't set myself a limit on price range, I was simply determined to be there, for both shows.

The Friday came, and at roughly 10 minutes to 10, I had two laptops logged into the website for the Glasgow venue and was preparing myself to enter the telephone number into speed dial, when a message popped up on screen notifying me that tickets would not be going on sale at present. Confusion doesn't cover it - had he cancelled? Was this a hark back to 1987 and a problem with licenses etc? It had been a very hasty announcement - perhaps too hasty?

As the story unfolded, it appeared that tickets were already being offered for sale on secondary (and legal) ticket sites for up to 20 times their face value and Prince and his people took umbrage to this. I am no fan of this method of ticket redistribution, due to the fact that it all appears above board, but I did feel that whilst Prince was doing the correct thing, this could have been avoided, and handled a lot better. Prince promised to reschedule the dates once the ticketing arrangements had been rectified. Sadly, that night, there was an atrocious and shocking terrorist attack during a concert in Paris where tragically, lives were lost. Following this, Prince revised his immediate outlook and put any overseas concert plans on hold.

Prince did play some shows in this format early in 2016, and the reviews he was receiving were akin to the 'Hit n Run' tours. My thoughts were very firmly that he would return to the UK and do more concerts - how could he not? Sadly, there was to be a good reason, which was not to be anticipated.

Three years to the day since Darran and I experienced the concert of a lifetime, we are attending another performance together - the Pet Shop Boys are playing a show in Edinburgh, Darran's hometown. It's a great performance, a bit more sedate than our experience of three years previous - We are seated in the theatre venue. Inevitably, we discuss the Prince show and our emotions that night. The Pet Shop Boys perform, as part of their set a track 'Vocal' - a section of the lyric parallels the experience of any gig (I suspect it may have been written in reference to more club music based events), but particularly the night of February 22nd, 2014,

I like the people, I like the song
This is my kind of music
They play it all night long
I like the singer, he's lonely and strange
Every track has a vocal, and that makes a change

Being at a Prince gig was where I felt true to myself - It was my kind of music, my kind of people (generally). Prince was my kind of star.

Jam 10 - 'Goodbye'

Tribute events are arranged swiftly post April 21st, 2016. The record listening collective I attend announces its intent to play 'Sign O the Times'. Unfortunately, this falls on the same night as Adam Ant playing a venue around Newcastle which Darran and I already have tickets for. I speak to Steve the organiser and genial host of the Record Player event and he kindly asks if I could put a few words together as an intro for the album. I think it is the focus of this event that sees me start to make progress with the loss of Prince. It's almost as if I go into some form of minor creative overdrive - I'd like to think similar to the way Prince operated in making an album, as unlikely as that comparison is.

My favourite cinema in Newcastle (coincidentally where 'The Record Player' is staged) announce a showing of 'Purple Rain' in one of its larger theatres (in fact, this is such a well-received event, a second showing is hastily added). It is nice when attending these events to talk to fellow fans, some of whom I know from the 'Controversy' days and hear that they are suffering too. I won't lie, watching 'Purple Rain' on a big screen is hard, but I feel I need to do it - I need to be there, if for nothing else than to represent myself. The song 'Purple Rain' unsurprisingly provokes tears - it is the centrepiece of the film and an emotional song at the best of times. It's multiplied tenfold now, more so given the performance Prince gives on film, which I must have seen hundreds of times, yet it emotes me even more, and still does. The first showing had some enthusiastic audience members, and it does become tricky to manage this - I will concede that 'Purple Rain' isn't high art, and is, to some degree, an extended concert video, but it was also hugely influential on me, and Prince's breakthrough, so can people please respect that some of us want to watch the film and reflect? The issue is taken out of my hands, as someone from the audience asks the perpetrators to keep quiet, which doesn't provoke further incident. The second showing is much more respectful, and I attend this on my own, and am able to sit away from anyone else...No one sees my tears.

Further events follow, and, I attend these out of duty, more than desire. A pub in Newcastle announces a 'Prince night'. I go, again alone, but don't venture inside. I can hear the songs being played, and it is a warm night in early summer. As well as the music coming from the bar, I can hear a drunken sing along. I don't want to hear this, so leave after around 25 minutes.

'Purple Rain' is shown again at a new venue in Newcastle. This time Darran attends. The promotion for the event promises, along with the showing, a Prince disco, live music and Prince related food. This event has been staged wonderfully, with recreations of scenes from the film (albeit tongue in cheek), and large Prince prints on every seat. However, I feel uncomfortable - despite Darran being with me. I fully get the angle that this should be a celebration, but to me, there comes a point where I feel a line is crossed and there is a tacky side to the evening. Maybe it's the fact that I'm not drinking, maybe it's the fact that it's too soon. A large part of me does question how many people would have attended such an event if Prince were still alive. One big factor is the attire which a lot of party goers have adopted.

There are a lot of attendees (mainly men) who are not in great physical shape yet decide that an ill-fitting purple shirt and an afro wig, is not only a good look, but also is a fitting representation of Prince. This to me is bordering on the 'fat Elvis' look that is so popular with Presley impersonators, despite Elvis only really looking that way for a small portion of his life. From one angle, this will seem extremely po-faced of me, but, again I don't want to be in a room of poorly thought through Prince look-alikes, in very much the same way I wouldn't want to be in a room full of strangers telling me what a great bloke my dad was - I know how good a bloke he was, and I know how much Prince meant to me. I don't plan to go to any further events.

It has always been a tradition, that, during the festive period, I would play a selection of my seasonal favourites at some point. ('Last Christmas' by Wham!, 'December Song' by George Michael, 'Christmas' by 'Low', the Elvis Christmas album, and 'The Power of Love' by Frankie Goes to Hollywood'). The Prince contribution to this festive pop platter is provided by 'Another Lonely Christmas' - the B-side to 'I Would Die 4 U' and an absolute tragic heartbreaker delivered by Prince. The song talks about Prince losing the love of his life (through death) on December 25th. Delivered with a vocal reverb that resonates with each line, this is almost a counter Christmas song, and feels, like many of Prince's lesser known songs; wasted as a B-side. Presumably, it was thought (probably correctly) that the song wouldn't get much airplay if released as a single, and it wouldn't really sit easily within the 'Purple Rain' album, but, at least it did see the light of day. Amazingly, there are a few different versions of the song, which I wasn't to appreciate until four or five years after first hearing the song. Additional lyrics, slightly different takes - both added to the intrigue of this sad, sad song.

This first Christmas without Prince, I can't bring myself to listen to the song - It is one of Prince's more bleak songs, and to try and imagine Christmas without Prince is hard. For many years I had received Prince related gifts at Christmas - records/CD's, books, posters, calendar's, DVD's, T-shirts (even more collectable items such as tour programmes and passes...and a framed sound wave of 'Purple Rain') - all devoured and appreciated. This year I ask for some of the items I haven't bought, and I gratefully receive them, as well as a couple of surprise additions. This all feels 'normal' until I suddenly realise he isn't here, and some of these items are now only available because of his death. Bittersweet with a sour taste. Not surprisingly, there is a new compilation released in time for Christmas by Warner's - '4ever' has a great cover photo and does a good job of pulling a lot of tracks from different eras together as representation/introduction to the Warner years. As with all compilations of this nature, there are a few 'odd' selections, and the edits of a lot of the tracks (for space economy reasons) don't do the songs justice. The big draw on this collection is the inclusion of the 'previously unreleased' 'Moonbeam Levels' - a gem of a track from the 1999 era. A piano based lament to writer's block, it is, in style, a close relation to 'The Beautiful Ones' and it is a true joy to hear a clear version of this heavily bootlegged song, which sounds very fresh, and at the same time, familiar, on CD.

Christmas Day 2016 gives a sad footnote to a sad year in music. George Michael, very much a contemporary of Prince in the 80's dies alone, suffering cardiac complications. George Michael and Wham were very much a part of my musical upbringing and George was an artist I admired, a lot. Prince clearly had an influence, and tracks on his 'Faith' album owe more than a nod to Paisley funk. There are comparisons with April 21st, and yet more tears are shed. This peaks with a car journey back from Boxing Day shopping, where the full length version of 'Purple Rain' is played on the radio at the end of a broadcast by Bryan Adams. I hold myself together, until the vocal improvisation following the mesmerising, emotional guitar solo - the section of the track that seems to break my heart every time. I cry for George, but mostly, for Prince. My wife, who is driving, notices my failing attempts at holding back the tears and places her hand on mine...Prince may have never meant to cause any sorrow, but his passing, and that of George Michael, has done just that, and whilst it isn't 'Another Lonely Christmas', it becomes a sad one.

As is the way, December brings end of year reviews in newspapers/online/on television. 2016 has had some large newsworthy events and has seen a number of high profile deaths. In 12 months, the world of music has lost David Bowie, Prince and George Michael, three very different, but also quite similar iconic male singer songwriters. All of the end year reviews feature all three to some degree. An interesting column takes a view that people should get over these deaths and stop mourning people they never knew. I see this point but disagree. I never met Prince, but his music and live performances moved me. He also inspired me, in more ways than I possibly admitted to. I understand life should go on...but so will my readjustment to a world without Prince. On the last day of the year, my wife presents me with a book about Prince which was meant to be a Christmas gift (the perils of online ordering!!) This was completely unexpected, but a touching gesture.

Earlier in the morning I listen to a recording of a 'Prince tribute' from a commercial radio station. I expect this to be a predictable montage of Prince's hits, and sure enough, it begins with 'When Doves Cry'...except this is the full length version - rarely played on radio, yet alone a commercial station. This grabs my attention. The show is presented by comedian Nish Kumar and is far from my expectations. Nish explains how he came to find Prince's music, in the early 00's (Prince wasn't exactly at his creative/commercial peak at this point) and rapidly familiarised himself with Prince's vast back catalogue. There is genuine feeling in Nish's delivery, and he tells a very vivid story of his experience of seeing Prince live at the O2 arena in 2007. Nish also conveys a point I feel I have been striving to articulate for some time - every fan he has spoken to about Prince feels that Prince 'belonged' exclusively to him/her - I can feel myself saying 'yes, yes' to no one, as I am in the room alone. Prince had an uncanny talent in making you feel as if he was performing just for you - in amongst an audience of 15,000 people. I have seen many live bands/acts in almost 30 years of gig going - no one at all comes close to Prince.

2016 comes to an end - a difficult year in many ways, although not without positive experiences. 2017 begins, and, in a lot of respects it is a relief to start a new year. Not least is the fact that it is no longer the year Prince died.

Outro - 'Welcome to the Dawn'

Over the course of putting my thoughts about Prince together I have examined my experiences and relationship with Prince and how relevant and prevalent he has been in my life, and how that relates to his passing and the emotional effect that had on me. It's true to say, that, at times, I felt a connection with him, almost taking me to a higher place, spiritually, perhaps, - however pious and obtuse that may come across. His music and concerts guided me through some difficult periods in my life and helped me celebrate the good times. I have formed friendships based around Prince, visited venues I may never have done, largely due to concerts and record shops, as well as profiteering from a vast array of musical styles and philosophies thanks to Prince. There are traits in my character that I can map back to him, in a semi-romantic (arguably indulgent and self-fulfilling) way (I didn't, for example suddenly become mildly socially awkward just because I read Prince had that in his locker, although it did comfort me to know he also had this infliction). It therefore would be a fair conclusion to expect to be upset, to some degree at the death of someone who fulfilled such an important role in my life. I completely get how ridiculous all of this may sound and read in print and, how, having never met Prince I shouldn't, rationally feel such personal grief. But I do. I still struggle listening to one of his most famous songs, 'Purple Rain' as it does feel that the sadness contained has undertones of a self-fulfilling prophecy - he may have never wanted to cause any sorrow, or pain...but his death did. As with most grief and upsetting experiences, time helps to heal, and I do feel a lot more able to listen to his music and discuss his impact than I did in the early weeks and months post April 21st, 2016. It comforts me that the last album he released in his lifetime is an extremely strong one. 'Hit n Run Phase 2' may not have a classic cover, and does contain a lot of tracks that had been floating around the Prince universe for some time, but it is consistent and includes the adorable 'Revelation' which appears extremely reflective, although not as much as the tear jerking 'Way Back Home' from 2014's 'Art Official Age' where Prince talks through his aspirations and going back to the place he belongs. As much as I wouldn't want to think he had predicted his own death, this track could be read as an end of a journey and a passing into another life - as I understand is the Jehovah belief.

It's clear I'm not alone in my sadness, and the feeling that we have lost a major innovative, forward thinking, genre breaking cultural influence, and that people still find it hard to refer to Prince in the past tense. His life appeared to be full of generosity and creativity, and, as banal as this sounds, brilliance. In terms of his recording prolificacy, Prince's last few years were amongst his highest - Four albums in just over two years - he finally had the control he yearned for, and each of these four albums had more than enough merits to be released (ok, perhaps Hit and Run Phase 1 had some ill-advised ventures into current dance orientated music, but it kind of worked on a 'mix tape' level) and each included more than one outstanding composition. There was also the re-release of the classic albums on repressed vinyl that was scheduled before his death. There was certainly enough high profile releases to keep Prince in the public eye, even before the Piano and a microphone tour announcements. His death kept his profile high, for more different reasons - the initial shock, the rumour, the mystery and the ongoing discussions over what happens next with his estate and his mass of unreleased tracks. Tributes to his talent continue, during award ceremonies - the Grammys and even the Brits have reflections on his death (and sadly, many other major musical icons that were lost in 2016). His albums are with us forever - he will never leave my heart and he will always be with me on a level. I will continue to be thankful that I was lucky enough to be of an age and time where Prince could have this level of impact on my life. Prince opened a lot of doors for me, and made it feel ok to express emotions openly, while still being aloof, distanced and uncomfortable in scenarios that were unnatural. This is me, very much influenced and guided by my family, but also by Prince Rogers Nelson.

Following Prince's death, I retreated from music - not intentionally, but more out of stunned shock - Prince was (and is) music - he defined my very belief in the medium, and with him gone, was there much point in going on? It became almost a question of religion, of existence in a huge part of my life. It would be some two - three weeks after his death that I could bring myself to listen to a Prince album, and even then it had to be on my own in a darkened room. Going to see a band/live act was equally something I couldn't comprehend and cancelled some previously planned gigs. The exception to this was Adam, playing 'Kings of the Wild Frontier' in full. I had looked forward to this since it was announced the previous year, and, given that Darran was travelling down from his home in Edinburgh, this seemed a very appropriate time to attempt to move on. Adam was great that night, and, just as it had done 36 years ago, a new musical chapter was beginning. Six weeks had passed since Prince's death. The shock was probably over, but the grief, far from it.

When Prince passed away, part of my confidence in life went with him - I had always felt whatever troubles or problems I had, would be taken away by Prince - whether it be a concert performance, a video, a look/style, song or album - It made me feel that he would in some odd way sort out my problems, directly or indirectly telling me everything would be ok, in the same way that some people turn to religion, I would turn to Prince and his music. He became part safety blanket - a world away from working class life in Newcastle, but a world I could be part of - an escape route, for however long or short I could stay - it affirmed my desire to dream and made the more humdrum aspects of the world, in the main, tolerable.

April 21st, 2017. It is now a year since Prince left us. The first year after any loss is the hardest. The subsequent years aren't easy. The lead up to the one year milestone (I've never been keen on the term 'anniversary' in this context as it implies celebration of the day a person died) and there is an abundance of activity relating to Prince, variable in content and context. Prince's first wife, Mayte, publishes her book and appears in the British press. She was once very close to Prince, and they had a child together, which due to extremely distressing circumstances, ultimately contributed to their separation (the baby died 8 days after he was born). I feel no desire to read this book but do share Mayte's sadness. Equally I have no desire to attend events that are being staged in Newcastle or watch what appears to be a poorly executed docu-drama about Prince's life which is shown on UK TV. I'm sure there will be a detailed Hollywood biopic of at least an aspect of Prince's life, sometime in the future. Now is too early and the trailer I see for the TV film makes me cringe and looks as though the production has been rushed. Darran confirms that the film is probably not worth watching.

What is intriguing is that documentary on BBC radio has a number of key players in the paisley world being interviewed. Susan Rodgers and Susannah feature, and give some insightful, revealing back stories to aspects of Prince's persona - the affirmation that he didn't sleep a lot, perhaps comes as no surprise, but when it relates to his creativity and Susan explains how constantly Prince recorded and sequenced albums, but then might change the album completely, whilst on tour playing arena shows, followed by small club after shows purely on adrenaline.

Susannah talks towards the end of the broadcast about how profoundly Prince's death has affected a close circle of people and how they are struggling to unravel the darkness. Susannah also brings into question the often quoted belief that 'Nothing Compares 2 U' was written about her. Sometimes you can hear too much!

I find comfort and empathy from Susannah's words - I am not in that close circle of people, and, go back to reiterate that I am and only ever was a fan, a big fan, yes. Possibly not the biggest - I am sure there are Prince fans who got him from 'For You' and saw him constantly up until the 'Piano and a Microphone' tour, which would pale my eight concerts and two after shows into insignificance. There are, doubtless, fans with a more extensive collection of memorabilia and can recite many more facts that I can. That doesn't matter to me - It's not a competition. I have stories of the experiences I have had, which have involved Prince, but moreover, I am so moved by Prince not being here as I have concluded that his influence has been very prevalent in my life - It may not always be obvious, but I know it is there. A simple example - I don't like having my photograph taken. I appreciate it has to happen sometimes, and sometimes I like looking at the photographs (my favourite photograph is one of my wife and I on our wedding day, kissing in front of the paintings where we were wed), but generally I don't enjoy it - This maps back to Prince, who made it acceptable in my eyes to say no to being snapped, and to follow your instincts and not comply. He is everywhere part of my job involves recording the frequencies of medication taken by patients involved in clinical trials. One of the frequencies is 'as needed' - this is termed 'per required need' or 'PRN' as an abbreviation...There he is again! Of course, I recognise that Prince only allowed so much of himself to be consumed, and the traits of mine which I map back to his are, fundamentally conjecture.

As the '21st' approaches, I reflect back over the year, and look beyond. Very interesting is the 'release' of a new Prince E.P. 'Deliverance' was recorded in 2006 and the studio engineer Ian Boxhill, has put the E.P. of six songs up for release on April 21st. Previews of the track are offered, and I can't help myself with this - I need to hear it. The full track isn't available, but excerpts are. Listening to the track sends a shiver down my spine - it's that same thrill of hearing his voice crystal clear on a new song and for a second I forget he's dead, and I feel a lump in my throat. I am brought back to reality when the excerpt ends. A momentary lapse of reason? Something more profound? The track certainly has a spiritual leaning, and it is quite extraordinary that this recording has been kept under wraps until now. Ultimately the release is blocked by Prince's estate. The astute business head of Prince is still prevalent!

The day of April 21st starts as any normal day, just as it did 12 months ago. I choose to play some Prince music today - it sees the right thing to do. I choose 'Parade' to accompany my walk into work. Inevitably, there are tears, but controlled tears 'Sometimes It Snows In April' may have surpassed 'Purple Rain' as the track most associated with Prince's death, given its prophetic aura and overarching sadness. 'I often dream of heaven and I know Prince is there', I whisper to myself towards the end of the track as my tears stream. The route into work is quiet and calm, not warm and sunny, not cold and storm like. 'Springtime was always my favourite time of year' 'Now springtime always reminds me of Prince's death' - 'Always cry for love, never cry for pain'. As I am listening to the album on my MP3 player, the album finishes, then goes onto to the next title - a bootleg recording of one of the Purple Rain live shows...I am instantly transformed emotionally, and I become entranced with the build up to the first song of the concert. I remember how excited I was at this point each time I saw Prince live, and the enjoyment those performances gave me. I feel subdued, and I watch the clock go around that evening...5.58pm there it is. 'This time last year'. The phone doesn't ring tonight - I don't get text messages, the television news doesn't contain reports of his death. Lorraine and I attend a basketball match that evening, which is very entertaining. I think of the basketball hoop during the 'Lovesexy' live show...There he is again.

During the past few months I have been in touch with a friend who I knew had moved to New Zealand, and I had not communicated with for some time. Via the medium of the electronic mailing format, it is great to be able to share news, reflect back and compare musical tastes. This leads me to recommend 'Sign O the Times' as an essential purchase to him. The album that represents the antithesis of Prince during his regal period. It gives me great warmth to hear that the album is purchased and enjoyed by my friend. Exactly 30 years since I got the album, people are still getting it. This must be part of Prince's legacy, and perhaps it's something I should take on as part of spreading the word. Prince may not have the same relevance in people's lives as he did mine, but his music can still be discovered and appreciated by new fans, young and old. Prince may have felt like he was just for me, but he wasn't. He was meant for everyone - He had mass appeal. It may have been a narrow mass appeal (he was never going to be Michael Jackson) due to his struggles with record companies and his creative output, and constantly evolving musical palate. He may not have always have had the credit he deserved, but that seems to be changing. He's just not here to see it.

Thinking back to the origins of this journal, I asked myself whether it was right to feel the emotion I did (and still do) regarding Prince's death. I have explored the part he played in my life, for not just his music and performances, but also his style and character. I think it's fair to say he has played a significant role in my life - perhaps more than I have ever admitted. This, to some extent has been recognised by others, and not exclusively those closest to me. The days after Prince's death, I was comforted, to some extent, that people I run into, whom I may not have seen for a while, and other acquaintances say they thought of me once they had heard the news. Even almost a year after his death, a colleague from work whom I haven't seen for a long time, due to her maternity leave, engages in a conversation about his passing, and how I felt. It would therefore seem not unreasonable to feel emotion towards this loss. Maybe the deep impact was questionable - the disinterest in music that lasted 2-3 weeks, the apathy towards live concerts and the upset that seemed to go on for days which ran into weeks. This perhaps is over sensitivity - I am not ashamed of it, but I didn't plan it. I never thought I would feel this way, but in all honesty, I didn't, for one moment ever think I would see the day that Prince died. It felt like he would go on forever, and possibly that is the real shock - He was mortal after all. We all die. There is part of me that recognises the grief is a metaphor for the grief I have kept bottled up for my dad and my grandma. Huge figures in my life, and perhaps due to functionality and priority I have been unable to truly let my emotions go. All good things they say, never last. And love, it isn't love, until it's passed.

A lot has changed in the way I view my relationship with Prince and his music. He is still very much in the public eye and his music is played on the radio/television - I don't give out a high pitched scream when one of his songs comes on the television, rather a resigned wry smile, coupled with a big intake of breath and a bit of lip biting. Sometimes I want to cry. Most times I don't. I can listen to his music and watch his concerts, but it is tinged with sadness. The joy is still there, only it is now frequently eclipsed with sorrow. I do feel this has improved, as it should - time is the key. I've touched on the realism of this situation and, on occasion, I do feel slightly self-indulgent on feeling this way - There are people who are losing parents/partners and children on a daily basis - this is real loss, not a pop idol you admire from afar. I reiterate - I didn't plan any of this.

The love of his music and the impact he had on my life will never leave me, my collecting continues (this will, I feel, never stop). There have been multiple events in Prince - time, since those innocent days in 1984 when 'When Doves Cry' first caught my attention, There now appears something that I am duty bound to do - visit his hometown, Minneapolis. See at first hand First Avenue, the 'Purple Rain' house, buy records from 'Electric Fetus' where he shopped. Go to Paisley Park, look at his playground, experience that aura of his residence, the place he created his magic and observe the urn that contains his remains. Darran and I have discussed this and feel it will give us a sense of closure. It will be a pilgrimage - a visit to hallowed ground, and will mean sacrifices along the way, but it is the only logical step remaining.

Paisley Park is in our thoughts and sights, as well as our hearts.

Rest in peace Prince Rogers Nelson - 4ever in my life

Appendices

Mr Drayton's Record Player is a light entertainment venture based on the communal experience of listening to a vinyl album. Located at the Tyneside Cinema and assorted other esteemed venues across the UK, the events are presented by Mr Drayton (Steve) and offer a variety of musical tastes, with accompanying facts and prize quizzes.

Mark and I took a punt on one of the first of these evenings when the album on offer was 'Ziggy Stardust and the Spiders from Mars'. I was so transfixed by the invigorating experience of listening to a complete vinyl album, in company, that I went back the next week, for the less well known (to me) 'For Emma, Forever Ago' by Bon Iver. From that moment I was hooked and was galvanised by the warmth offered by the group (in particular, genial host Steve, whom I have struck up a firm friendship with) and found myself enjoying many more albums on vinyl, which coincided with that medium's profile.

The Record Player has played two Prince albums and incorporated the 'Purple Rain' film into its offshoot project 'Mr. Drayton's Movies and Munchies'. I feel very fortunate that I have worked with Steve on the Prince themed Record Players and also presented the 'Kiss' single during a 'singles club' Record Player. Included are two pieces I contributed

Sign 'O' The Times - Album Playback Speech: 01.06.16

Since Prince's sad and unexpected passing, I have been struggling to cope with listening to his music, any music, going to gigs, general life functions.

With this in mind, I decided to seek some medical advice. I went to see the doctor and guess what he told me. He said 'boy you better try to have fun no matter what you do...But he's a fool...

Sorry about that...It is true that Prince's passing really has upset me, and it does feel a bit odd almost delivering a eulogy here...but at the same time, it gives me the perfect opportunity to celebrate unquestionably the greatest popular musician of my generation and my own personal hero. I'm delighted Mr Drayton and the Tyneside have joined forces to play my favourite album of all time - Sign O the Times.

Released in March 1987, it was Prince's third album in three years, since Purple Rain had made him a global superstar. Some of the songs here had been knocking around from as far back as 1982, and ultimately were collated from three projects Prince was working on in 1986 - those being the Revolution based band collaboration 'Dream Factory', which was pulled when Prince disbanded the Revolution. Alongside this, Prince was working on a much more funk based solo release using studio manipulated vocals to create an androgynous alter ego called 'Camille' – This proposed 8 track album was expanded and ultimately became the triple album presented to Warner's 'Crystal Ball' - None of these projects officially saw the light of day, although illegal copies are available at selected car boot sales.

Warner's and just about everybody else simply could not keep pace with Prince's creative output and were reluctant to release a triple album. This is significant as, in denying these ambitious releases, the relationship between artist and record company started to deteriorate. So, Prince went away, trimmed down/collated/added a few more tracks and Sign O the Times as a double album was the end result. This is my copy, bought on the day it was released in the bag it was purchased for the sum of 7.98.

More than any other of his albums, this is Prince experimenting with a whole range of his musical influences and the sounds available to him - the Linn Drum is present, but so is the energy of James Brown, the guitar rock god of Hendrix, the gospel of the Staples Singers and the pop of Sly Stone all mixed with a sprinkling of P-funk and an overriding Jazz feel.

The album is a sheer tour de force and testament to one man's innovative musical kaleidoscope of ideas, whilst remaining an incredibly coherent collection. It is often hailed by critics alongside 'What's Going On' and 'Songs in the Key of Life' and has been mentioned as the last great double album of the vinyl era. Lyrically, there are themes of love, sex, religion and fun, all of which Prince had explored previously.

Opening with lead single and the title track, we get Prince's stark reflective narrative on the wrongs of the contemporary world. Almost as soon as its last beat has played out, we're into the kick back party anthem 'Play in the Sunshine' - Just as on 1999, Partyup and LGC Prince is encouraging us to forget the gloom of the world and party to the max.

Four separate singles were released from the album - all of which made the top 40 in the UK. One of the most unconventional love songs ever is 'IIWYG' - it pushes gender boundaries in a way no one else had before or has since, played out to a sparse slightly off funk beat with a killer bass. Prince sings in the Camille voice and then goes even higher/faster as the song reaches climax...and then silence... A memoir to a platonic female bond from a male perspective – this was based around Prince's observation of the closeness between twin sisters Susannah (whom Prince was briefly engaged to) and Revolution guitarist Wendy Melvoin. It also provided confusion to the masses... including some of my classmates at school who, completely missing the point, had Prince down as a "bender" ... The irony...

Given its vast tapestry of musical styles, it is hard to categorise this album - psychedelic art funk Minneapolis style is about as good as I can do. Maybe the best way to place this album is to say it is a Prince album, which itself became a genre... But not just any Prince album...the best. Prince would go on to release more great albums at an increasing pace, but nothing quite as expansive, creative and as off the wall as this. It's fitting we remember him this way, for the musical genius he was.

Thank you, Prince.
I wish U heaven

Kiss - Prince and the Revolution

I bought this single in 1986 from 'Hitsville USA' - a now defunct record shop in Old Eldon Square, not far from here. The shop was notable for many things, not least of all for its carrier bags which had the strap line 'A funkin good record store'. Or, if you were sat at the back of Mr Fisk's Geography class and had a red biro and some Tippex, you could come up with something a little bit more creative.... Snigger.

Whilst thumbing through the 'Soul Classic' section one wet Saturday afternoon, a mate and I stumbled across a white 7-inch cardboard sleeve with the words 'Prince - Kiss' written across it in black marker pen. This took us somewhat by surprise as between us we had all of Prince's back catalogue...Plus, Smash Hits hadn't mentioned anything in its gossip column.

Upon quizzing the 'friendly' assistant, we were informed that this was 'his new single and wouldn't be released here for a couple of weeks'...so after a quick recky of the pennies in our Geordie Jeans pockets, we each purchased a copy...even at the then extortionate price of £2.48... Well, it had come all the way from America. However, as we had spent all our money on our prized purchases, we had to walk home... Luckily, we saw the funny and funky side.

The song itself comes from the album 'Parade' - subtitled 'music from the motion picture Under the Cherry Moon' - It was originally written for one of many of Prince's protégée bands 'Mazzerati', but, legend has it, upon hearing the bands version, Prince reclaimed the song, twiddled with it a bit and the rest is history...But just to show there were no hard feelings Mazzerati do receive credit for the backing vocals on the single!

The single reached Number 6 in the UK charts, Number 1 on the Billboard Hot 100 in the US and was voted single of the year by NME in 1986. For me, it represents Prince at his playful, teasing, flirty, funky, creative, sexy and camp best. The song sits equally within the context of the album, the film and as a single in its own right, and I'm incredibly grateful to Mr Drayton for allowing me to share it with you... Just don't tell Prince as we might have a lawsuit on our hands...

Mr Drayton's Record Player presents 'Purple Rain' (album playback, November 2012)

Cake made by my wife for communal enjoyment during the album playback

Live sets

For pure self-indulgence (and future reference) I have included the set lists of the concerts I attended (sourced from internet, although I can't - 100% guarantee the accuracy).

Wembley Arena, London: 3.8.88 (Lovesexy tour)

Erotic City
Housequake
Slow Love
Adore
Delirious/Jack U Off/Sister
U Got the Look
I Wanna Be Your Lover
Head (with George Clinton)
When You Were Mine
Just My Imagination (Running Away With Me) (The Temptations cover version)
Little Red Corvette
Pop Life
Controversy
Dirty Mind
Superfunkycalifragisexy
Bob George
Anna Stesia

Intermission

Eye No
Lovesexy
Glam Slam
The Cross
I Wish U Heaven
Kiss
Dance On

(Piano set)
When 2 R in Love/Venus de Milo/Strange Relationship
Condition of the Heart/Raspberry Beret/How Come U Don't Call Me Anymore
The Ladder/Do Me, Baby (with "When 2 R in Love" reprise/coda)

Encore:
Let's Go Crazy
When Doves Cry
Play Video
Purple Rain
1999

Encore 2:
Alphabet St.

Wembley Arena, London, England: 10.7.90 (Nude tour)

The Future
1999
Housequake
Kiss
Purple Rain
Take Me With U
Bambi
Alphabet St.
The Question of U
When Doves Cry
Ain't No Way (Aretha Franklin cover version)
Nothing Compares 2 U
Batdance
Partyman

Encore:
Baby I'm a Star

Maine Road, Manchester 21.8.90 (Nude tour)

The Future
1999
Housequake
Kiss
Purple Rain
Take Me With U
Don't Make Me Pay for His Mistakes (Z.Z. Hill cover version)
Alphabet St.
Venus de Milo
Under the Cherry Moon
The Question of U
When Doves Cry
Do Me, Baby
Ain't No Way (Aretha Franklin cover version)
Nothing Compares 2 U
Batdance
Partyman

Encore:
Baby I'm a Star

Meadowbank Stadium, Edinburgh: 29.7.93 (Act II)

My Name Is Prince
Sexy M.F.
Love 2 the 9's
The Beautiful Ones
Let's Go Crazy
Kiss
Irresistible Bitch
She's Always in My Hair
Raspberry Beret
Sometimes It Snows in April
The Cross
Sign "☮" the Times
Purple Rain
And God Created Woman
Little Red Corvette
Strollin'
Scandalous
Girls & Boys
7

Encore:
1999
Baby I'm a Star
America

Encore 2:
Come
Endorphinmachine

Encore 3:
Johnny (The New Power Generation cover version)

G-MEX Centre, Manchester: 10.3.95 (The Ultimate Experience)

Endorphinmachine
The Jam (Graham Central Station cover version)
Shhh
Days of Wild
Now
The Most Beautiful Girl in the World
P Control
Letitgo
Pink Cashmere
Loose!
I Love U in Me
7

Encore:
Get Wild (The New Power Generation cover version)
Get Up (I Feel Like Being a) Sex Machine (James Brown cover version)
Gold

The O2 Arena, London, England: 4.8.07 (21 nights/Earth Tour)

Let's Go Crazy
Take Me With U
Guitar
Shhh
Musicology
Pass the Peas (The J.B.'s cover version)
Play That Funky Music (Wild Cherry cover version)
Sexy Dancer
Le Freak (Chic cover version)
I Feel for You
Controversy
What a Wonderful World (Louis Armstrong cover version)
Cream
U Got the Look
If I Was Your Girlfriend
Pink Cashmere
Lolita
Black Sweat
Kiss
Purple Rain

Encore:

Little Red Corvette
Raspberry Beret
Sometimes It Snows in April

Encore 2:
Crazy (Gnarls Barkley cover version)
Nothing Compares 2 U

Unable to obtain setlist for after show at IndigO2 - Prince appeared but played guitar only for brief spell (?5 mins)

The O2 Arena, London: 16.9.07 (21 Nights/Earth Tour)

Chelsea Rodgers
Misty Blue (Eddy Arnold cover version)
Baby Love (Mother's Finest cover version)
1999
I Feel for You
Controversy
Somewhere Here on Earth
If I Was Your Girlfriend
Musicology
The Question of U
The One (The New Power Generation cover version)
What a Wonderful World (Louis Armstrong cover version)

Piano set
Adore/Insatiable/Money Don't Matter 2 Night/Dear Mr. Man
I Would Die 4 U/Little Red Corvette/Under the Cherry Moon
Love Is a Losing Game (Amy Winehouse cover version)
Cream
U Got the Look
Take Me With U
Guitar
Whole Lotta Love (Led Zeppelin cover version)
Kiss
Purple Rain
Encore:
Nothing Compares 2 U

Sampler set
Sign "☮" the Times/When Doves Cry/Alphabet St.
Irresistible Bitch/Darling Nikki/Pop Life/I Wanna Be Your Lover
The Most Beautiful Girl in the World/Raspberry Beret

IndigO2, London: 17.9.07 (early hours after show)

Thank You for Talkin' to Me Africa (Sly & The Family Stone cover version)
3121
Girls & Boys
Delirious
Song of the Heart
Satisfied
Beggin' Woman Blues
Lolita
Black Sweat
You Bring Me Joy (Mary J. Blige cover version)
Nine Million Bicycles (Katie Melua cover version)
Gotta Broken Heart Again
Sing a Simple Song (Sly & The Family Stone cover version)
Everyday People (Sly & The Family Stone cover version)

Manchester Academy, Manchester: 22.2.14 (Hit and Run: Part 1)

Let's Go Crazy (Reloaded)
Guitar
Plectrum Electrum
FixUrLifeUp
Something in the Water (Does Not Compute)
When We're Dancing Close and Slow
She's Always in My Hair
Funknroll
Sign "☮" the Times
Hot Thing
Forever in My Life
I Could Never Take the Place of Your Man
Crimson & Clover (Tommy James & the Shondells cover version) (w/ Wild Thing chorus)
When Doves Cry
Alphabet St.
Nasty Girl (Vanity 6 cover version)
777-9311 (The Time cover version) (Bass solo)
Housequake
I Would Die 4 U
If I Was Your Girlfriend
(instrumental)
Purple Rain

Encore:
Screwdriver
Chaos and Disorder
How Come U Don't Call Me Anymore
Starfish and Coffee
Diamonds and Pearls
The Beautiful Ones
Under the Cherry Moon (instrumental)
Venus de Milo
Sometimes It Snows in April
Nothing Compares 2 U

Encore 2:
The Max
Play That Funky Music (Wild Cherry cover version)
Encore 3:
Take Me With U
Raspberry Beret
Cool (The Time cover version)

Encore 4:
Endorphinmachine
Bambi

Encore 5:
Colonized Mind
Cause and Effect

Songs played from tape
Pretzelbodylogic/Stop This Train

'Acknowledge me.'

I was very reticent in sharing my thoughts with anyone, and it took me some time to feel comfortable about talking about something that may become 'a book'.
Naturally, it was my wife I first confided in. Lorraine was a huge support through the period of Prince's death and my subsequent mood of sadness and withdrawal. Lorraine may not have agreed with my methods, but her acceptance and love (which continues) is something I will never forget. I truly feel blessed to have such a caring wife.

As a youth, my mother (mam), dad, grandma, grandad and sister provided me with the platform to explore the world of Prince. They may not have understood, but (my sister apart) rarely teased me for my fanaticism. My parents continued to fund this fascination and my mam especially was creative and helped make dreams turn into reality.

I'm not someone who has ever classed himself as having a lot of friends. Music has always provided many hypothetical friendships. I don't bond easily, but when I do, I become close to those around me. The friends I have are incredibly special to me. Darran, my oldest friend and my confidant in all things Paisley has experienced most of the ups and downs of being a Prince fan with me. I'm lucky that Darran can recall almost as much as I can, and I thank him for his unsung contribution to my story.

Mark Q, Mark W, Steve and, latterly David have all helped in more ways than they could ever imagine - reading over drafts and formulating constructive criticism, as well as offering ears that listened - thanks to all of you. Michael made sure the stops and caps were where they should be - OCD, does come in handy, sometimes!

Finally, none of this would have been possible without the musical genius that was Prince Rogers Nelson. The Beautiful One. Love and respect.

Made in the USA
Lexington, KY
09 May 2018